Get
Your
Kids
HIKING

Get Your Kids

How to Start Them YOUNG and Keep It FUN

HIKING

Jeff Alt

BEAUFORT
BOOKS

Library of Congress Cataloging-in-Publication Data
Alt, Jeff.
Get your kids hiking : how to start them young and keep it fun / Jeff Alt.
    p. cm.
ISBN 978-0-8253-0691-4 (pbk. : alk. paper) --
ISBN 978-0-8253-0651-8 (ebook)
1. Hiking for children. 2. Family recreation. 3. Outdoor recreation.
I. Title.
GV199.54.A58 2013
796.51083--dc23

                         2012044819

For inquiries about volume orders, please contact:
Beaufort Books
27 West 20th Street
New York, NY 10011
sales@beaufortbooks.com

Published in the United States by Beaufort Books
www.beaufortbooks.com

Distributed by Midpoint Trade Books
www.midpointtrade.com

Printed in the United States of America

Interior design by Elyse Strongin, Neuwirth & Associates, Inc.
Photos by Jeff Alt and John Mitchell
Photo design by Emily Felger
Cover design by Tobias Design

Contents

8: See You in a Few Days!
Backpacking with Kids

9: Think Food! Think Water! Think Fun!
Tips and Menus for Drinking and Dining Out, Literally,
on the Trail

10: No Bites! No Burn!
Keep Your Kids Safe from Bugs and Sun

11: Becoming a Seasoned Hiking Caregiver
Some Skills and a Little Knowledge Can Go a Long Way
on the Trail

12: Everything but the Kitchen Sink!
Clothing, Packs, Footwear, Sleeping Bags, Stoves, and More

13: Hike with a Team
Utilize the Amazing Services and Resources Offered by
Our Parks and Trail Associations

14: Not Me, but Us
Thoughts for Seasoned Hikers and All Caregivers
Hiking with Kids

Get
Your
Kids
HIKING

Give Your Kids Those First Steps on the Trail

And You Will Give Them a Skill and
a Healthy Habit That Will Last a Lifetime

Much research has emerged in the last decade about the physical and mental health benefits of walking. Walking is increasingly recommended by doctors for cardiovascular health, weight loss, stress relief, and as a supplement for treatment of depression. Take all these good traits of walking, add in the rejuvenating outdoor views and the escape from the hustle and bustle, and it really becomes clear to me why hiking is one of the healthiest sports in which you can participate. Here is what hiking does for me:

+ Hiking keeps me fit. Not only do walking and hiking strengthen your muscles and joints, but they're also good for maintaining a healthy weight. I also lose a noticeable amount of weight when I hike for extended periods, even though I eat enormous amounts of food. Nutritionists will tell you that if you walk all day in rugged terrain while carrying a pack on your back, you could potentially burn four thousand to six thousand calories a day, the equivalent of running two marathons. Furthermore, because regular exercise increases a person's immune response, I also have more energy, and I don't catch colds or fall ill easily when I'm hiking routinely.

* Hiking brings about my most positive thoughts and conversations. This is not surprising, since doctors explain that exercise increases the endorphins in the brain and relieves stress, resulting in a euphoric state of mind.

* Hiking inspires my creativity. The natural, simple, and profound outdoors is the perfect place to let your mind be free. Recreation experts and business consultants will tell you that when you remove yourself from the hustle and bustle of your routine, the pressures of your normal environment fall off your shoulders. I've learned that I can think outside the box when I am actually physically outside the box.

* Hiking helps lighten the pack of life. It's easy to get bogged down in our daily lives by taking on extra responsibilities, spending more time on work projects than with family, and running in all directions without a focus. Hiking helps me regroup and separate my priorities from the responsibilities that I've

shouldered. It's amazing how much more refreshed and successful I am after I realign my focus and goals.

Children have the most to gain from all the great benefits that hiking offers. By introducing your kids to hiking, you are helping them take steps, literally and figuratively, in the right direction.

Childhood obesity is at an all-time high. Research shows that most children will be exposed to some level of computer activity and TV by the age of two. This early exposure to electronic entertainment, as well as the trend of housing and shopping centers replacing undeveloped forest and farmland, has led many children to prefer video and computer games and TV to playing outside. Sloth-like indoor play is competing with a good old-fashioned romp in the natural outdoors. I've come to realize that it's our role as parents to help our children appreciate the simple things that only nature can provide.

Parents and caregivers play a critical role in introducing children to outdoor playtime at a very young age. What you do with your child in the first few years of life has a tremendous impact on his or her future habits and development. In fact, ninety percent of a child's brain is fully developed by five years of age. Young children are physically and mentally taking in everything they are exposed to. It's no coincidence that a child responds best to therapeutic intervention at these young ages (early intervention) if a child is at risk of a developmental delay. Given this evidence, it stands to reason that if you start your youngster out in the outdoors, they will embrace it as the norm later in life.

The best way to introduce children to the outdoors is to make it fun. Play is how kids learn. When something is fun, we want to do that activity again. Involving kids in fun, engaging outdoor activities will instill a desire to continue playing outside. Even within an environment of computers and television, kids will associate fun with playing outside, and the electronic gadgets won't be their sole form of entertainment.

The simple yet profound outdoors offers an opportunity for our children to play, exercise, and grow in a natural way. As our landscapes become more and more developed for commercial or residential purposes, our local, state, and national parks and forests are quickly becoming the main resources for our children to discover the wonders of nature. Our parks play a critical role in nurturing an appreciation for the outdoors in our children, and I encourage you to explore all that your local parks can offer. Then, expand your horizons to include state and national parks, both near and far. You will be teaching your children both a lifelong love of the outdoors and an appreciation for the incredible beauty of our country! As a seasoned outdoor family, we've been hiking with our kiddos since they were born.

Raising children is an adventure in itself. Knowing where to begin, how to plan and prepare, and how to make hiking with your children fun shouldn't be a mystery. I've compiled my tips and advice on hiking with kids into a step-by-step guide so that you can quickly and easily find the guidance you need for a specific age or topic. The faster you can find the information you need, the quicker you can hit the trail with your kids!

We all want to give our children an edge as they head out into the world. Guiding your kids step-by-step into the wonderful world of hiking will serve them well in the rapidly changing environment in which we live. Introducing your child to a sport that can serve as a relaxation and thinking tool, while providing them with an inexpensive way to stay both mentally and physically healthy, is worth every step. Hiking is a sport that will endure a lifetime, one that they will never outgrow.

2

Start 'Em Young, Really Young

Hiking Fun with Your Infant: Birth to Six Months

Sharing the outdoors with our newborn daughter ranks right up there on my list of greatest and most rewarding adventures! When our daughter, Madison, was only two months old, my wife and I took her on her first hiking adventure to Red River Gorge in Kentucky. Bringing your child on the trail can be a rewarding adventure, but it does require some planning.

Becoming proud parents of a newborn baby is such an amazing and fun experience, and it goes so fast. Yet I must tell you that before our daughter was born, I had a fear of how my life was about to change. Before children, my wife and I routinely filled our packs with provisions and drove out of town on any given weekend, hitting the trail on a moment's notice, our only worries being about ourselves. We didn't have a dog or even a plant to care for, and there we were, about to have a child. As responsible parents, our child's needs would come first, before our own. Raising a child requires your A game. You don't get second chances. From the moment your child is born, how you raise him or her will impact everything else: who your child is and what he or she will become. Those first few months and years are the most critical. Despite all those concerns, as soon as I set eyes on our daughter and held her in my arms, my fear of parenthood melted instantly away.

Those pre parenting years of hiking had prepared me to take my children on the trail of life. My wife and I had already experienced firsthand what the simple, yet profound, outdoors can do for your physical and mental well-being. Knowing our kids would be exposed to far more indoor, sedentary activities than we ever were as children made us realize that it was our role as parents to introduce our kids to the great outdoors as young as possible, before they would ever hold an electronic tablet or watch a television show. This way our children would know they can have fun outside hiking, splashing, running, smelling the fresh air, and spending time with family and friends—even more fun than they would have playing the latest computer game. Starting them this young would help them to grow up thinking this is how people have fun—outside. We added some child-friendly accommodations to our hiking routine and began taking Madison with us into the backcountry. Including her in our adventures enhanced our appreciation of the positive role the great outdoors can have on raising a child. It's extremely fun and easy to get your kids hiking, especially when you start them really young.

Establish a Routine

Children like predictable routines. As most new parents discover, infants respond best to a predictable daily schedule, which makes creating a daily hike with your little one easier than at any other time. Carving out a consistent time each day to take a hike or walk at the youngest of ages will have a positive impact in your future hiking success with your children. Allow yourself a thirty-minute daily window in which to "hike." The walk itself may last only fifteen to twenty minutes, but holding thirty minutes aside will allow time for putting on your shoes, bundling up, changing a diaper, and preparing your baby. Most mothers of newborns are eager to get back into shape, and walking with your precious little one is a great way to exercise. Check with your doctor and pediatrician to be sure you and your infant are ready for this endeavor before you begin.

This advice isn't just for moms, though. All caregivers can start a hiking routine. If you already have a walking time established, congratulations! You are well on your way to walking with your kiddos! If you participate in athletic endeavors outside of walking (running, team sports, going to the gym, and so forth), continue with all those activities but don't let them replace your walking schedule. The purpose is to establish an outdoor regimen that your *child* will come to accept as part of his or her day. This walk will also serve as training time for bigger adventures away from home, allow one-on-one time with your child, and give your kids daily exposure to the great outdoors.

If you keep your walking time as simple and practical as possible, you will be more likely to stick to it. Avoid time-intensive preparation and making elaborate, detailed plans that would require stressful scheduling with others. Find a time of day that will not interfere with other activities, and keep this time sacred. Don't give this time up, with the exception of occasional, unavoidable intrusions (e.g., bad weather, illness, and the like). Don't give up if you miss a day or two. Just put one foot in front of the other and get back on track. If you can maintain a walking regimen five days a week, you and your baby will reap the benefits of fresh air and exercise.

Until your walking routine has become a habit, keep visual reminders. Write your walk time on a wall calendar; post it on the refrigerator, on a dry-erase board, and anywhere else in your home that will remind you to walk every day. Stick to your daily walk and it will become easier each day. Your walk will become a healthy habit. Children crave routine, and your healthy walking habit will be easy to instill in them. Tie a daily errand or responsibility into your walk, such as walking the dog, walking to the post office, visiting a neighbor, and so forth. Knowing that you have to retrieve your mail or take your dog for a walk will give you added incentive to get up and out.

Prepare for Your Adventure

Walking is the simplest form of exercise that there is. In most cases, you simply lace up a pair of shoes, put one foot in front of the other, and walk! However, you will need some gear even for a neighborhood walking program, and some or all of this gear can be used for any hiking endeavors outside your neighborhood. Hiking requires some essential gear, which we will cover in more detail later. Walking and hiking are essentially interchangeable terms, although hiking typically involves a trip beyond your neighborhood. The items listed below are the basic items to get you started on your walking program. Review the appendixes for complete gear lists.

Necessary Equipment and Gear List

+ Infant carrier such as a BabyBjörn, or a sling. Infants and children under six months should be carried in front of you using a carrier or a sling. Features and age limits vary from brand to brand.

+ Sturdy pair of shoes. Running or walking shoes will work well for pavement and grass. If you plan to walk on trails, you should invest in a pair of trail shoes with a heavy sole that can absorb the impact of stepping on rocks and other debris.

+ Moisture-wicking or wool socks. Non cotton athletic socks will help to prevent blisters and keep your feet cool in the summer and warm in the winter.

+ Moisture-wicking synthetic shirt and pants or shorts

+ Rain jacket

+ Hat

+ Quart-size water bottle or a hydration hose system

* Snacks

* Day pack

Some Secondary Gear

* Stroller (umbrella or jogging)

* Trekking poles

* Pedometer

* Sunglasses

At this age, a child carrier is recommended instead of a stroller. The child carrier allows you to bring your little one anywhere your feet will take you, on or off the road. Strollers are restricted to paved and relatively flat areas. Carrying your infant snug against your body is more natural for your little one, who has spent nine months in the womb. However, if you don't have access to a child carrier, a stroller will provide a means of walking with your child, and it is better than not going at all. A stroller will play a larger role later on in the toddler years (covered in chapter 4).

Infant carriers are available from most retailers that carry baby products. Read the child-carrier manufacturer's directions carefully. Always make sure your infant has an open airway and can breathe without obstruction when you are carrying her. Be careful not to smother your little one with protective clothing or anything that could interfere with her breathing. Adjust your child in the carrier often to make sure she is getting good circulation.

Most infant carriers are made of cotton, and most baby clothes are cotton as well. In general, cotton is a big no-no when hiking. When cotton gets wet, it retains moisture. That can lead to chafing at best, and it can cool down your internal body temperature, leading to hypothermia at worst. Avoid hiking in extreme conditions like rain, snow, or very high or very low temperatures with your infant. Of course, weather is unpredictable, so play it safe, and whenever possible dress your little one in synthetic fleece or wool outfits. Try to acquire a non cotton carrier such as the newer Baby-Björn child carrier, which is available in a moisture-wicking, mesh design. Although some parents prefer cotton diapers for their environmental impact, disposable diapers are synthetic, and they are designed to wick moisture away from the baby.

Infants have sensitive skin. Consult with your pediatrician before applying any protective products on your infant. The American Academy of Pediatrics (AAP) recommends using sunscreen on children older than six months. Protect infants, six months and younger, with clothing and by avoiding the sun. The AAP suggests in the instance where you can't avoid sun exposure to apply only a minimal amount of sunscreen with at least SPF 15 to the exposed areas (face and hands). No bug repellents should be used on children under two months of age, and some repellents are not recommended until a child is at least three years. The AAP and the Centers for Disease Control and Prevention (CDC) recommend using repellents containing picaridin and DEET as the most effective agents to repel mosquitos carrying the West Nile virus and ticks with Lyme disease. These two active ingredients are recommended after a child is two months of age. Be sure to follow the product recommendations and make sure it is recommended for children. Avoid applying repellents to an infant's hands or anything that will end up in his mouth or make contact with his eyes.

Footwear, clothing, and day packs for mom and dad are available from your local outfitter. Most outfitters specialize in fitting customers into proper footwear, and they also sell the non cotton layered clothing that is recommended for hiking.

Money-saving tip: check with resale shops for child carriers, put a note out on your social network pages asking your friends for their hand-me-downs, or add these items to your baby-shower registry.

Keep Your Walk Fun!

If something is fun, you will want to do it again and again. This is true for kids and for adults. During these early months of hiking and walking with your infant, you want to make sure the walk is enjoyable for you, the caregiver. If you're having fun, you will be eager to hit the trail, and the positive energy will spread to those around you, including your infant. If your child knows you're enjoying your hike, he will feel more content as well. During these early months, hiking is your chance to focus on yourself, your child, and those close to you. Your walk can be your time away from all the distractions, worries, and pressures of new parenthood.

Tips to Keep Your Walk Fun

* Invite your friends, neighbors, parents, and your other children for a walk, but avoid making complicated, stressful plans.

* Your walk is a great time to rekindle your romance with your spouse without the distractions of home. As you walk, relish and celebrate the new addition to your family.

* Do you like plants and flowers? Route your walk in areas with beautiful gardens or flower beds.

* Are you into history? Discover your local history on foot. A quick Internet search will pull up local historical markers to explore.

* Walk with a purpose and a destination: Walk to your favorite restaurant, to the beach, or to the park. Plan a picnic along the walk.

* Participate in an organized walk or join a local walking club. You may meet new friends or contribute to a worthy cause or both.

* Continuously change your walking route. Variety keeps your walk interesting.

* Use a pedometer to keep track of your miles. Add up your miles and challenge yourself to walk the distance

of a marathon, the Appalachian Trail, or the distance Lewis and Clark traveled across the United States.

✤ Plan a future hiking adventure and use your daily walks to train and try out all your gear.

Help Your Infant Experience the Outdoors

Your baby is growing rapidly at this early stage. At first, you may have your infant facing you in the front carrier or sling to provide needed neck support. As your child's muscle control develops, you may face him outward to explore the world instead of facing in toward you. Children learn through exposure, using all their senses. Give your infant opportunities to explore nature safely during your daily walks.

✤ Find a patch of grass and let your child sit, roll, or crawl around.

✤ Let your baby touch leaves, pinecones, and any natural items in your immediate area, being watchful that he doesn't stick the items in his mouth.

✤ Let your little one splash his hands and feet in streams, lakes, and ponds, keeping him safely in your grip and being mindful of the current and depth.

✤ Verbally label items you see along your walk. Even though your infant may not be saying words yet, he is listening, and this will help him develop his vocabulary and language skills. When you hear birds chirp, say "Bird" or "Can you hear the bird?" while pointing, so your baby learns to focus his attention on the source of the noise. Maintain a conversation about the world around you with your baby.

Be creative. Everywhere you hike you will find new opportunities to safely expose your child to new objects, sounds, and vocabulary. You will be amazed at how much fun you will have experiencing the joy of your child's discovering things for the very first time!

Prepare for a Vacation Hike with Your Infant

Take advantage of the early months in the life of your infant to plan a longer hiking adventure. It could be to a state park, a national park, along the seashore, or to a waterfall or a mountain view. Wherever you desire to go, you can walk at your own pace while your kids are this young. This will also give you the incentive to use your daily walks to train for your upcoming adventure. After determining your destination, research the climate, terrain, distance, and dangers along the trail (such as animals). All this information will help you to acquire the necessary gear and to train properly.

An added benefit of having an established walking routine is that you're already conditioned to take on a more rugged hiking adventure. Do you plan on hiking eight miles a day? Have you walked this far carrying a child? A few weeks before heading out on your adventure, take some training hikes, simulating the distance and terrain you plan to navigate. Add the gear you will carry on a more remote hike in the woods, mountains, or beach to your daily walk. This will help you prepare and decide if your proposed endeavor is practical and reasonable, especially while carrying your child. Our daughter and our son were both carried in front carriers on extended day hikes along mountain trails in numerous parks before they were eight weeks old. Our daily walking routine prepared us.

Have a plan for inclement weather (rain, snow, excessive heat). Call off the hike if the weather forecast is not desirable. Save the hike for another day. Even though you packed along all the right gear (rain gear, cold weather gear, and so forth), infants are more prone to medical issues when exposed to extreme conditions than you are. Always err on the side of safety. My motto is to make every hike with my child a fun and memorable one, even at the earliest age. Slogging through mud puddles, fording dangerous rivers, having to build a shelter to weather out a storm, or any scenario that calls for the exclamation "We made it out just in time" or "That was a close call" is not on my list of things to do while hiking with my baby!

Avoid overnight hiking with your infant. All the additional baby gear (diapers, playpen, bedding) will weigh you down, and as the saying goes, "The lighter the pack, the more enjoyable the journey." Instead, establish a base camp at a car-accessible campsite, hotel, house, or lodge. This will allow you to be a parent, not a Sherpa. This will also permit you to bring along all the necessary equipment for your child. I know some hikers who have taken their infants on overnight hikes, but this is risky. Most likely, your hike will be uneventful, but even the healthiest infant is medically fragile. They are more prone to hypothermia and other illnesses. If a medical emergency were to arise, minutes count, and you might be too far removed from amenities to respond in time. Lean on the side of safety, and save the overnight hiking for the older child. I will cover overnight hikes in a later chapter.

Have an emergency plan. Carry a first-aid kit and brush up on child CPR and first aid. Learn the signs and symptoms of hypothermia and monitor your child for these signs. Be sure to pack your child's medication, including infant ibuprofen or acetaminophen, if your pediatrician recommends these. Acclimate yourself to the location of the nearest medical facility for children along your route. (See chapters 11 and 12 for a full list of considerations.)

Never hike alone. This is true for all hikers and especially true when hiking with children. You should always have another caregiver or adult with you when you hit the backcountry.

Always leave your itinerary with someone. Be sure to include your date of departure and return, your point of entry or trailhead, and park contact information.

Hiking with your infant sets a healthy foundation in place for you and your kids to build from. Your child is developing rapidly and this will become a valuable one-on-one time spent with your child. You should be able to carry your child in an infant carrier or sling until about six months of age. Some wraps and slings can be used beyond six months, so check the manufacturer's recommendations. This time will pass so fast. Enjoy every step!

OUR SECOND CHILD, William, was just six weeks old when we packed him up in a child carrier and took him out for his first hike: a day hike in the Shenandoah National Park (SNP). We took the Mill Prong Trail from Skyline Drive (mile 52.8) to the Rapidan Camp (also known as Camp Hoover). Our round-trip hike was four miles in length, and it was a sunny day with moderate summer temperatures. I carried Madison, who was nearly three, on my back, and Beth carried William.

Rapidan Camp was the presidential retreat used by President Herbert Hoover before Camp David was built. Most of the buildings have been restored, and in the summer months, the park coordinates guided historical tours. I love hiking and history, making this one of my favorite trails in the SNP. When we arrived at Rapidan Camp, William began to fuss, indicating it was feeding time. We searched around and found a secluded spot on the porch of the Prime Minister's Cabin for Beth to breastfeed William. Other than the birds' chirping and the distant burble of the Rapidan Stream, it was so quiet that we thought we had the camp all to ourselves. Beth was very modest and private about breastfeeding, so even though she was completely covered, when thirty people suddenly appeared on the porch as she fed William, I saw Beth's face turn shades of color I had never seen it turn before! The tour guide, not missing a beat, stated, "Mrs. Hoover loved children. This may have been a place one of her guests would have fed her baby," and the group went on its way. Beth's facial colors slowly returned to normal, and she continued feeding William. It was a parenting moment we will never forget!

John Mitchell, photographer

3

Precious Pounds on Your Back

Explore the Outdoors with Your Baby and Toddler: Six to Thirty-Six Months

Congratulations! You survived the first several months of parenthood, and hopefully by now you have some "hiking with little one" adventures under your belt. If you are just getting started on hiking with your little one at the six months to three years range, please review the suggestions for establishing a walking routine in chapter 1. To prevent injury and make hiking enjoyable for everyone, routine walks to condition yourself for carrying your little one are key. Even if you do have an established walking or hiking routine, I recommend that you train with your kids around your neighborhood before going out into the wild.

Six months to three years of age is a wide range with very visible and rapid growth. Your hiking adventures will become much more fun and interactive. At six months, your little one is not yet ready to walk, but she is more alert and developing rapidly. By now, your delicate little hiker is becoming more aware of her surroundings. She is absorbing everything around her. At six months, your little one will begin to sit up. Your one-year-old is likely standing up and will soon walk. Your two-year-old is probably walking independently, and your three-year-old is probably walking, running, and jumping. Your child's motor, speech, and language skills are also developing at a very rapid rate. Within this two-and-a-half-year time frame your child will begin saying her first words, and by the time she is three, she will be speaking in phrases and short sentences. This stage is an opportune time to instill in your child all the fun that can be had in the outdoors.

A video game or television program simply cannot replace the learning that can occur in the simple yet profound outdoors. On a hike or while playing outdoors, you can tap into all the senses that a child uses to learn. Just think of the sounds: birds chirping, brooks babbling, bees buzzing. The tactile sensations: splashing in a stream or ocean, digging in the sand, walking barefoot in the grass. The visuals: spying an eagle soaring across the sky, witnessing a deer eat grass, watching a squirrel scurry across a branch, seeing grasshoppers jump across a field. Each time you head outdoors, you are taking your little hiker on a fun adventure that will fill them with wonder for nature and will provide them with opportunities for learning and exercise.

At this stage, one of the biggest perks for the caregiver is that you can continue to hike at your own athletic pace.

Enjoy this time, as it allows you to cover more miles, getting in your workout and reaching that summit, view, or waterfall. During the six-month- to thirty-six-month stage, you will continue to carry your child, but your precious cargo will shift from your front to your back.

A child carrier fits a wide range of child growth, and if you're already conditioned to hiking with your infant, then the transition from the infant carrier to a child carrier will be seamless.

Acquire a Child Carrier

When your child has good neck support, around six months, he is ready to hike with you in a back-loading child carrier. He is getting too heavy to carry in front without risking injury to you. Some infant carriers adjust from front-loading to back-loading, but backpack manufactures have mastered the craft of designing packs to carry heavy loads safely on your back, with the bulk of the weight resting on your hips. So, who better to design a child carrier than a backpack manufacturer? Since there are several high-quality brands of child carriers to choose from, visit your local outfitter for this important purchase. Most outfitters have professionals trained in sizing and fitting you into a backpack or child carrier.

You want to be sure to select a pack that is comfortable for both you and your child. Many of the same considerations used to fit you into a traditional backpack for hiking—such as torso length, waist size, gender, and cubic inches of storage space—also apply to a child-carrier backpack. Most child carriers are designed for both genders to wear, but you will need to make some adjustments to the carrier when switching between male and female caregivers.

Child carriers have a harness system similar to a car seat's that allows for growth, but there are other questions to consider when selecting yours:

> Does the pack have a sun/rain/weather cover?
> Is the gear-storage area adequate for all your supplies?
> Does your child fit safely into the carrier?

You will use this carrier for at least the next two years, until your child is walking on his own or is too heavy for you to carry. If your child is three years old and you are just now looking at purchasing a child carrier, be aware that your child will outgrow the carrier very soon.

Money-saving tip: You may find a child carrier at a secondhand store or an online merchant, but the same considerations apply. If the pack doesn't fit right, at best you will be uncomfortable and not enjoy your hikes, and at worst you can cause injury to yourself and your child. Be sure you know what your specifications are before shopping online.

Once you have selected a pack, follow these additional guidelines:

* Always have an adult assist you in loading your child into the pack and saddling it onto your back.

* Follow the manufacturer's directions: Securely strap your child into the seat, making sure she is comfortable.

* Most packs have a hip belt, shoulder straps, load-lifter straps, and a sternum strap. Make sure that you fasten all of the straps available on the pack.

* The bulk of the weight of the pack should rest on your hips, not your shoulders.

* If the pack is pulling on your shoulders, then you will need to make an adjustment to the straps.

* If possible, have the outfitter fit you and your child into the pack and bring along your adult hiking partner so he or she becomes familiar with the pack.

* Be sure to use the sun/rain hood to protect your child.

* Even on overcast days, apply pediatrician-recommended sunscreen to your child.

* Never pack food or any scented items (sunscreen, toothpaste, and so forth) in the child carrier. Another adult hiker should carry any scented items so that if you encounter a bear or other animal that is in pursuit of food, your child will not be in danger.

* Try out hiking poles. They can help stabilize you as you hike and spread out the workout with the added weight of a child.

Continue Your Walking Routine with the Child Carrier

In chapter 1, I talked about the importance of establishing a walking or hiking routine. Once you select a child-carrier pack, be sure to add it to the routine. Children will react differently to being carried on your back, and the best way to help kids adjust is to make it routine. After just a few hikes on the trail or around the neighborhood, your little one should get used to their new perspective. This will also help you adjust to carrying the extra weight on your back. Even if you don't take regular walks or hikes with your kids, you should train with everyone in the weeks leading up to your hiking adventure. This will help you adapt to carrying the pack, and the kids will adjust to the routine. Your training hikes will pay off when you strike out on your big family-vacation adventure. You will be physically and mentally prepared for the endurance challenges.

As mentioned in chapter 2, always walk with a second caregiver. The second caregiver can tend to the needs of your child without your having to take off the pack every time your little one needs attention. Your child will have an elevated view, sitting with her head slightly higher than your own. Most kids enjoy this, as they get to view everything from the eye level of an adult. Your little one may even nod off to sleep to the calming rhythmic motion of your stride!

• • •

Acquire the Right Clothing and Gear for Your Child

❖ As mentioned in chapter 2, avoid cotton! Dress in layers, using only synthetics; fleece; wool; or waterproof, breathable items. (See chapter 12 on clothing.)

❖ Be sure to bring what you need for the weather conditions you will encounter.

❖ Make sure your child has water-resistant footwear. Until he starts hiking on his own, you can get away with typical toddler footwear, but be sure to avoid cotton socks.

❖ A wide-brimmed sun hat will help protect your child's face, ears, and neck from sunburn.

❖ Your little hiker is growing rapidly at this stage and will outgrow clothes as fast as you buy them. So it makes little sense to invest in high-end namebrand outfits until he is older. You can find synthetic clothing (polyester, fleece, wool) in the baby sections of most big-box stores. Some clothing such as rain suits (pants and hooded jacket) and wicking long underwear (top and bottom) may be available only from a specialty outdoor retailer. Avoid rain suits that have a cotton liner. If you do buy the high-end, brand-name rain suits and long underwear, buy them several sizes too big. You can roll up the pant legs and sleeves now so your child will get several years of wear out of one outfit.

Avoid overnight hiking with your toddler. We will cover overnight hikes in a later chapter.

Keep the Hike Fun!

Build excitement about your impending adventure before you go. Show your kids pictures of animals, plants, and objects you might see. Read books to them about the outdoors. Show them where you're going on the park website. Most parks have websites with pictures. Rent videos of places you want to go.

Take frequent breaks: As your child becomes more aware of her surroundings, let her touch and experience everything she sees, hears, and smells (within reasonable judgment). Stop frequently and get her out of the carrier. Let her crawl and walk around (in the grass, not poison ivy!). The older kids will want to get out of the pack more often than your younger child.

Tie items to the pack using shoestrings or rings to keep your child entertained. Your little one can pull the item of interest up into the pack and push it down when done. Some fun and practical items include the following:

- a pacifier

- play binoculars

- play compass

- books (choose books related to the outdoors)

- a favorite small toy

Hike only in nice weather. Make every hike a sunny walk in the park, even if it rains. If the forecast calls for rain, extreme heat, or frigid temperatures, call off the hike. Have an indoor backup plan. You want your child to have fond memories of your adventure. Hiking in only fair weather will help build those fond memories. Storms can arrive unannounced in the great outdoors, so always be sure to have all the right essentials to keep everyone safe, warm, hydrated, and dry. If you get caught in a storm, keep a fun, calm demeanor while you work your way out of the backcountry. This will convey a safe and even fun message to your little one.

Make replenishing with food and drink fun. Pack your kiddo's favorite snacks and plenty of water. The fun food will encourage your child to eat for energy. Kids love snacks. Stop every ten or fifteen minutes and have everyone take a sip of their water. Stop for an extended relaxing lunch along the trail.

Kids like to sing, and music helps them learn. Sing songs as you hike along. Kids love rhyming songs. If you have a musically talented caregiver or child on board, bring along that harmonica, flute, or guitar. Use discretion when others are on the trail seeking tranquil quiet, watching birds, or enjoying observation of animals.

Talk to your child about what you're seeing. Label animals, objects, and sounds as you encounter them. Expand your child's language as you walk. No two children develop exactly the same. You will need to adjust your level of language to what you feel is appropriate for your child. Here are a few examples of fun language activities you can do with your kid as you walk along.

* 6- to 12-month-old child
    * Label plants, animals, sounds, and objects as you encounter them.
    * If your little hiker verbally approximates the name of something as you're strolling along, praise her and repeat the word she attempted. ("Yes!" "Bird." "Good job.")
    * Whatever object or sound your little one shows interest in, make that your topic.

* 12- to 24-month-old child
    * Ask your child to point to items you name (tree, rock, bird).
    * Continue to label plants, animals, sounds, and objects as you encounter them.
    * Repeat and expand on words and phrases. For instance, if your child says, "Bird, Mommy!" you could say, "Yes! That's a bird. It's a hawk."
    * Play I-spy or I-hear games:
        – "I hear the wind. Do you hear the wind?"
        – "I spy a big rock. Do you spy a big rock?"

* 24- to 36-month-old child
    * Ask your child to label plants, animals, sounds, and objects as you encounter them.
    * Expand on whatever your little one talks about. For instance, if your child says, "Look, Mommy! Deer!" you could say, "Yes! That's a baby deer!"
    * Play I-spy, I-hear, or I-feel games:
        – "I see something that is green and hanging on a tree." Give extra clues if needed. "That's right, it's a leaf."

– "I hear a loud whistle. That's right, it's a bird chirping."
– I feel: Put an item in your child's hand. Ask her what it is. Ask her how it feels. Give her the vocabulary to describe it. ("What is this? It's a rock. How does it feel, hard or soft? It's hard.")

Potty Training in the Woods

If your little one is potty training, incorporate that into your hike. Encourage your child to go potty just as you would at home. Every time you need to go to the bathroom, model how to go using good backcountry, leave-no-trace methods. Find a spot at least two hundred feet from the trail and waterways and dig a six-inch "cat hole." When you're finished, bury all waste in the cat hole. If possible, dig the cat hole near a tree, log, or large rock to give you something to lean on. Some of us may not have good balance without a pot to sit on! If your toddler is still in diapers, pack along all the items you usually carry in your diaper bag (diapers, wipes, hand sanitizer, a small changing pad, tissues, trash bag). You will need to pack out the used diapers with you. For this reason, you should bring along an extra trash liner. You can dispose of your child's number two the same way you dispose of your own in the woods. Bury the contents of the child's diaper in the cat hole, and put the dirty diaper itself in your trash and carry it out. Be sure to review the backcountry bathroom recommendations for each park and area in which you're hiking. Some areas are extremely fragile.

When your little hiker surpasses thirty-six months, she will begin to develop enough coordination to start hiking on her own. You will know when the child-carrier days are coming to an end when you find yourself walking down the trail, following your child with an empty child carrier on your back, or when she is so heavy that you find it cumbersome to carry her.

MY WIFE AND I embarked on our first lengthy expedition with our daughter and extended family out of the United States—all the way to Ireland! We trekked over fifty miles with our twenty-one-month-old daughter and four-year-old nephew. Our journey was a far cry from a death-defying feat up Everest, but in order to include our child in our adventures, we knew we had to tone down our usual pursuits until our child was older. It was worth every step.

We trekked the Burren Way, which had a haunting *Lord of the Rings* feel, with ancient grass-covered hills speckled with medieval granite, Disneyesque castle ruins, and remains of roofless stone peasant huts overgrown with chest-high grass. For six days we followed trail markers snaking along farm lanes lined with rock fences, most certainly the same paths the medieval Celts once traveled. With the Atlantic Ocean and distant islands in view, we trekked along the massive, breathtaking Cliffs of Moher and over rock fences through cow and sheep pastures. We bedded down in cozy family-run B and Bs and dined in pubs, eating Irish beef stew, fresh battered cod, and smoked salmon.

The Irish lived up to their hospitable reputation, shuttling us into town for dinner, carting our dirty laundry to the cleaners, and cooking up a very hearty Irish breakfast each morning. Having lodging at the end of the day allowed us to rid our pack of dirty diapers, get out of the unpredictable lashing wind and rain, maintain our child's bath routine, and bed her down in somewhat familiar sleeping quarters.

My wife, Beth, carried all of our clothes, snacks, and amenities in her backpack, which defied the laws of physics, crammed beyond capacity. Beth beamed from ear to ear when she learned that the B and Bs would portage her backpack ahead to the next night's lodging.

The first day of our journey, we stopped along the path to change Madison's diaper. I laid down my rain parka and placed a diaper-changing pad on top. After putting a fresh diaper on Madison, we secured her in my pack and, once again, hoisted her on my back. As we began trekking down the path, Beth had some pep in her step and a smile on her face. We had walked about fifty yards down the trail when Beth realized she had left her backpack where we changed Madison. It was a good thing Beth wasn't carrying our daughter, we joked, as Beth ran back and retrieved her pack.

Madison enjoyed the entire journey. She was perched high on my back, with a half-circle weather cover propped over her. She was amused by the horses, mules, and cows that would stick their heads over the rock fence, like Mr. Ed. She learned to play the harmonica as we trekked along, and she read a book tied to the side of the child carrier. Our routine hikes prepared us for this adventure, and our entire family had a great time.

4

Child-Directed Hiking

Discovering the Trail with Your Preschooler:
Three to Four Years

By your child's third birthday, your approach to hiking will shift to a slower pace. You've reached a point where your child has mastered the ability to walk and run without falling down every few steps. By now, most children will lose interest in riding on your back, but even if your child wants to ride in the carrier, he is now at a weight that can strain even the most athletic adult. Now is the time not only to let your child's interest lead your walk but also to let it set the pace. I call this child-directed hiking. This can be a big adjustment for some, but it's well worth it. It may require you to find an alternate workout to supplement your decreased physical activity by exerting yourself on a run, walk, or hike at another time. Don't be discouraged by the slower pace. This is an important step in nurturing your little one's growth into a competent hiker.

Your new mantra: The goal is not reaching the summit, view, or waterfall but for your little one to have such a fun time that he wants to hike again and again. At this age, hiking, whether it's on a mountain trail or around your neighborhood, should be all about having fun and exploring the outdoors. So, if stopping for an hour to play in a creek after walking only a few hundred yards makes your child happy, then you had a successful adventure that will lead to many more! At first, you may stop every few feet to explore a rock or a bug or to splash in every puddle or creek you encounter. As your child continues to develop his endurance, he will naturally hike farther, and eventually he will be giving you a run for your money up to the summit. For now, don't push it. Keep it fun. Make every outing an adventure he will never forget. What you may find amazing is how much more *you* enjoy the simple pleasures of your child's exploration. There is something very satisfying when your child is having a ball in the outdoors, splashing her feet in a stream, looking at the pill bugs under a rock, or counting butterflies.

Put yourself in the shoes of three- to four-year-olds. They like to play and have fun. They have great imaginations. Supply them with the right equipment for their adventure. A few simple inexpensive items will add miles of fun to your child's hiking.

• • •

Acquire an Adventure Pack

Now that your little one is hiking on his own, outfit him with an adventure pack and let him fill it with gear. You don't need an expensive high-end pack; a school backpack or knapsack will do the trick. This will allow your little one to bring along his own items to add to the adventure.

Select a few practical items for your child's adventure pack that he will use, such as a water bottle, binoculars, a magnifying glass, a kids' camera or throwaway camera, a hiking tool with a compass and whistle, a flashlight, a map, and a bug catcher. Let your little adventurer pack a few items of his own. This will give him a sense of ownership. Even if the item is unrelated to the outdoors (a car, a doll, a stuffed animal), let him pack it along, unless it's too big or heavy to fit in the backpack.

It's Time for Comfortable Footwear

Now that your little hiker is walking down the trail, get her properly fitted in a pair of comfortable trail shoes with a sturdy sole. The selection of footwear for kids at an outfitter is slim at this age, so you may need to look at your favorite shoe store. Since it may be difficult to find shoes made specifically for hiking at this age, a good pair of running or gym shoes and non cotton socks will do the trick. If you can find hiking shoes, look for a sturdy sole (I recommend Vibram, if available), with waterproof, breathable fabric (such as GORE-TEX). If you can't find waterproof, breathable footwear, just be sure the shoe or liner fabric is not cotton.

Acquire the Right Clothing for Your Child

As mentioned in previous chapters, avoid cotton and dress your child in layers (synthetics, fleece, wool, and waterproof/breathable items). Be sure to bring what you need for the weather conditions you will encounter. (See the appendixes for gear lists and clothing.) A wide-brimmed sun hat will help protect your child's face, ears, and neck from sunburn. (See chapter 12 for more details about clothing.)

The Child Carrier and the Folding Umbrella Stroller

If you already have a child carrier, don't get rid of it. On longer excursions, your little one may get fatigued and need to be carried out of the backcountry. You may find yourself carrying an empty child carrier as your three-year-old transitions to hiking, but you will be glad you brought it along when your little one loses her energy. If you don't have a child carrier, don't invest in one at this age. It will hardly get used.

Although many trails don't allow wheeled devices, an umbrella stroller can come in handy for a fatigued child. The adults can take turns carrying the stroller until it's needed. It folds up and can be pulled along by two wheels or it can be strapped to a backpack. This type of stroller is inexpensive, lightweight, and surprisingly durable. You can push it along gravel and hard-packed dirt and around camp, and it is compact in comparison to most other baby and toddler equipment. If you don't have a child carrier, this is a great option for when your preschooler gets too tired to walk. Just be sure to use it only on the trails that allow wheeled devices.

Base Camp

Avoid overnight hiking at this age. Save that for the older child. Overnight backpacking with your preschooler can be done, but you will add unpleasant pounds to your pack, and you will need to disperse your child's gear among the older hikers, which will weigh everyone down. You may still have to carry around dirty diapers if your preschooler is not yet fully potty trained. I recommend establishing a base camp at a car-accessible campsite, hotel, house, or lodge. Car camping will allow your little one the opportunity to enjoy the camping experience, which will help her prepare for the overnight backpacking excursion later on. A base camp will allow you to be a parent, not a Sherpa. Having a base camp will also allow you the ability to coordinate some additional activities to get in your full workout. You can leave your group safely at your base camp and get in an extra hike or more exercise on your own, if needed. You can take turns with other caregivers watching over the kids.

Keep the Hike Fun!

Get your preschooler excited about his adventure before you hit the trail. Research the destination with your child. Show him pictures of your destination on the park's website. Check out books from the library about the area you plan to explore. Show your child pictures of the animals, terrain, waterfalls, and other things you will see. Let him pack his own adventure pack. You will be amazed at the excitement created when a little one gets to pack for his adventure.

Once you start your hike, keep the fun activities going.

Make up rhymes and songs. Stop and explore using items from his adventure pack. For example, look under rocks for bugs or look at a leaf up close with the magnifying glass. Take pictures of things you discover along the trail, such as pretty flowers, mountain views, or butterflies. The pictures will give your child a visual reminder you talk about your adventure when you get home. Stop for snacks and a drink. Break out the Goldfish crackers or whatever snack your little one prefers. Take frequent hydration breaks. Every fifteen minutes, stop and hand everyone his or her water bottle. Make sure everyone takes at least a sip. Take your kids on a guided nature walk with a naturalist or a park ranger. Park staff really know how to engage children. You will be amazed at all the facts you'll learn as well.

As you walk along, play preschool learning games with your child such as I Spy and ask her questions to help her explore the nature around you. Be sure to add detail in your explanations and descriptions of the adventure.

- ✦ "I spy something that is . . ." (square, green, round, a rectangle, and so forth).

- ✦ "I spy something in the sky. I spy a black bird. It looks like an airplane."

- ✦ "Does the bark feel smooth or rough?"

- ✦ "Everyone stop, close your eyes, and listen for three different sounds." Go around the group and ask each kid to name what they heard.

✤ "How many different colors do you see?"

✤ Use who, what, where question games such as the following: "What animals do you think live in the park?" "What shapes do you see? I see an oval green leaf." "What do you hear? I hear a bird chirping. It sounds like a whistle." "When I step on the leaves, what does it sound like? That's right, *crunch*."

Coming up with fun activities for your preschooler is as simple as looking at what she is learning at school. If she just learned about shapes, pick out different shapes of items in the woods. Whatever skill your child is learning, add it to your outdoor repertoire. If she is counting, count the trees. If she is learning about patterns, point out the patterns of leaves, bark, or moss on the trees. If she is learning about respecting others, teach respecting the outdoor habitat. Reinforce good backcountry ethics. Take nothing from the woods but pictures and memories. Model picking up litter you find along the trail.

Your little adventurer's confidence will build with each hike. Your activity list will grow with each stage of your child's learning. She will begin peppering you with questions as she discovers the outdoors. If you don't know the answer, admit it, and then together look it up or consult with the park staff. This will help give your preschooler the confidence to one day explore and find answers on her own.

• • •

Potty Training in the Outdoors

Three is the magic age at which many children master the skill of using the potty. Refer to chapter 3 for more details on going potty during a hike. Encourage your child to go potty on your hike just as you would at home. Every time you need to go to the bathroom on the trail, model good backcountry ethics. Carry biodegradable bath tissue. Review the backcountry bathroom recommendations for each park and area you're hiking in. Some areas are extremely fragile and may have a "pack everything out" policy.

I WAS ON a short hike with my four-year-old son and seven-year-old daughter in the Great Smoky Mountains National Park. We were about a mile into our walk when I realized that I had to use the bathroom. My kids had just used the potty before we hit the trail, and my wife had run ahead to get in her cardio workout for the day. Following good backcountry ethics, I needed to find a spot at least two hundred feet from the trail and the nearby stream. The trail was rated easy and was heavily populated with other hikers that day, so I also needed to go off the trail far enough to be out of view.

I instructed my kids to follow me as I navigated the way off the trail a good distance so I would be out of view. My son wanted to ask me a question, and I told him to wait until I was done going to the bathroom. I told my kids to stop about twenty yards from my chosen spot behind a tree. Once I finished my business, I began to lead my kids back toward the trail.

At that point, my son asked in a whisper of a voice, as if he were about to share a secret, "Daddy, you know our 'Take a Hike' song?" William was referring to a song we sing during a skit we present about family hiking. Each lyric is a tip on hiking as a family. I wrote the lyrics and my brother arranged it into a folk bluegrass song.

"Yeah, what about it?" I replied.

"You know how we sing, 'To prevent from getting lost, stay on the trail'?" William asked.

"Yeah," I responded, wondering where he was going with this.

"Well, we're not on the trail!" William stated in a matter-of-fact whisper, making his point that we were breaking the rules that he had memorized in our song. He was whispering because he thought we were breaking official, national park rules!

I laughed as I realized he was technically right. We were not on the trail. I didn't include going to the bathroom, an exception to the cardinal rule of staying on the trail, in the "Take a Hike" song. As I explained to William that going potty is one of the few times we leave the trail on a hike, I realized the power of a song for teaching children. William had remembered every word to our "Take a Hike" song, and he was hiking by the rules.

5

Adding Miles

Covering More Ground with
Your School-Age Hiker: Five to Twelve Years

The ages of five to twelve years old are ripe for lots of family hiking adventures. By your child's fifth birthday, your little hiker should be able to walk independently and accomplish short round-trip excursions (one to three miles), and her ability will increase with each passing year. A physically active twelve-year-old can easily carry a backpack and hike distances comparable to an adult hiker's. Your child's ability will vary depending on how much physical activity she is used to. Kids that take regular hikes and walks, or who are involved in youth sports, will have more athletic stamina than a child who gravitates to sedentary activities such as video games, television, and the like. A child who's been acclimated to hiking at a younger age will also tend to be more enthusiastic about taking a hike than a child who has primarily been entertained by indoor activities. Make no mistake about it—in today's technological age, your hiking adventures are in direct competition with the latest video game when it comes to grabbing your child's interest and enthusiasm. Instead of trying to compete against technology, incorporate a few high-tech gadgets into your adventure to win over your tech-savvy child. The goal at this age range is to continually engage your child with hiking adventures that are so fun she will want to hit the trail again and again.

The five- to twelve-year-old stage is an exciting time to head out on many family hiking adventures. As the adult caregiver, you are still carrying the bulk of the load (food, equipment), but your five-year-old is now capable of carrying some items in a small pack. You no longer have to lug along extra baby equipment. You don't have to pack diapers or carry out the dirty ones in your pack any longer. You most likely aren't stopping every few yards, and your child should be showing interest in hiking to that waterfall or up to that mountain view. She now has the physical ability to reach those destinations, within reasonable distances. Now that your kids are traveling at a more enduring length and pace, you may even be able to get in your own full workout while hiking with your children. This age range is a special time to instill your core family values while you are removed from all the distractions of a busy domestic routine and before your kids become teenagers.

If you're like me and enjoy the solitude of the woods, carrying everything on your back and surviving without electricity or hot showers for days on end, your kids are now at the age where you can plan an overnight backpacking trip. However, overnight backpacking isn't for everyone. You can still enjoy hiking in the great outdoors without sleeping in a tent and carrying everything on your back. Most national parks and forests, as well as state and local parks, have modern amenities, within reach of some great trails. So don't let your distaste for going without a shower get in the way of hiking with your school-age hiker. I know many people, including my own extended family, who will hike with me at every opportunity until I say, "Let's camp." Please refer to chapter 8 for details on how to prepare for an overnight adventure in the woods and how to make it a success.

Now that your child is capable of heading out on more extensive adventures, you need to make sure she has the right gear. Many of the same equipment decisions that you make for your own adventures can be applied to outfitting your children.

Acquire the Best Footwear for Your Kids

As your child increases his miles, good footwear becomes more essential than ever. Be sure to get him properly fitted in a pair of shoes that will be comfortable and can withstand the ruggedness of your adventures. Hiking boots and trail shoes may be scarce for the five- to seven-year-old, depending on your locale, but your luck in finding good trail footwear will increase with your child's age. As mentioned in previous chapters, be sure the footwear fits well and, as always, avoid cotton socks. See chapter 12 for tips on selecting footwear for children.

Acquire the Right Clothing

Kids are growing at a rapid rate in the age range of five to twelve, which makes investing in top-of-the-line, name-brand clothing an expense with little return on investment—unless you have other children who can wear the garments your older child outgrows. Fortunately, the non-cotton type of clothing that you need (synthetics, fleece, wool, waterproof/breathable rain parkas and so forth) can be found at most big-box discount stores. As mentioned in previous chapters, avoid cotton clothing and dress in layers (base—undergarments; middle—shirt/fleece/pants/shorts; outer—rain parka/wind pants/gaiters). See chapter 12 for gear tips and lists of clothing items for kids.

Acquire the Right Backpack

By the age of five, the adventure fun pack has run its course. If your child can wear a school book bag, he is ready for a backpack that can hold real provisions. Your five-year-old will still want to bring a toy or two along, in addition to his "real" provisions. You can get away with a school backpack for the five- to seven-year-olds, with lightweight loads, but you will want to acquire a more durable, hiking brand of pack with a hip belt, sternum strap, and hydration hose capability for the older child. See chapter 12 for specific tips on shopping for the right pack.

• • •

Assess Abilities

A hiking adventure involves physical exertion, and you need to be sure your kids are prepared. Five to twelve years is a wide age range, and you should assess your child's abilities to determine what he is capable of handling, in terms of the distance you will walk, the pack weight he will carry, and the climate in which you will hike. A good gauge to help determine your child's physical abilities is to look at his other athletic pursuits. Are your kids involved in extracurricular sports? How far is the coach having your child run? How long will your child play on the soccer field before tuckering out? What experience does he have with hiking? Is he involved with Scouts? Do you take daily family walks? This will help you plan your adventure based on your child's outdoor knowledge and capabilities. Does he carry a book bag to school? The weight of his book bag will give you a starting point as to how much weight your child can realistically carry, at least for short distances. This information will help you match your adventure to the capability of your group, and it will help you develop a training program if you are planning a big trip that involves distances and terrain for which your family is not quite prepared yet. The child-directed hiking technique from the previous chapter still applies at this age. You want to plan an adventure that your child is able to complete, and more important, you want him to have fun doing it! You want him to feel successful about his accomplishment. Plan a hike within reason, keeping the slowest and youngest hikers in mind.

Training hikes, also known as shakedown hikes, will help you and your family get ready for your adventure. To really get a feel for your kid's capabilities, take a test hike around the neighborhood or around your local park. Use all your hiking equipment and carry the pack weight you plan to bring on your actual excursion. Set a distance that you think everyone in your family is capable of completing. Pay close attention to the attitude of the group. Assess how everyone did and be as objective as possible. What worked and what didn't? Were there complaints about ill-fitting gear? If the footwear, pack, or clothing doesn't fit, exchange it at the outfitter before you leave on your excursion. Did everyone hike a distance comparable to what you plan to hike on your trip? Was the terrain similar to the excursion you are planning? If everyone did well, this will be a confidence booster. If the training hike was more like a forced march, you may need to cut back on the distance and spend more time training. Continue to get outside every day. Save money by not driving everywhere—walk to dinner, to the grocery store, and to the library. Make walking as routine as brushing your teeth. The more your family walks, the easier it will be to hike to that view or waterfall, and the more fun everyone will have.

Keep the Hike Fun!

Making your outings fun is essential to maintaining interest in hiking at this age. Remember, you want your children to have such a good time on each hike that they want to do it again and again and again. Planning and preparing can be part of the fun for this age group. Kids in the age range of five to twelve like to be a part of something. Make them feel important by letting them play a role in the adventure planning. Older kids can use the computer to research your destination or sport. All US national parks and most state and local parks have websites chock-full of facts and information. Attend local slide shows or lectures (at outfitters, libraries, and bookstores) about your excursion every chance you get. Send for maps and guidebooks of the area, and check with the local travel experts on hiking, rangers, guides, and the like. Have the packages sent to your child or children; receiving mail will only add to the excitement! Bring the outdoors inside. Educate constantly to generate interest and enthusiasm. Get magazines, videos, puzzles, and artwork that show places you want to go. Rent movies about faraway places. Use the Internet together to look at maps and photographs of the wildlife, environments, and spectacular scenery you will be visiting someday. While on your adventure, take lots of pictures of the kids and places you go. Enlarge photos of your adventures to display in your home as a reminder of your fun times.

Go high tech. Bring on the gadgetry! Turn your video gamers on to adventure technology. Explore all the possibilities—from a global positioning system (GPS) and a pedometer to headlamps and flashlights to apps for smartphones and other mobile devices. Investigate how these incredible devices are being used for fun on the trail, like scavenger hiking in the Shenandoah and Great Smoky Mountains National Park (see Kat and John Lafevre's *Scavenger Hike Adventures*), geocaching, letterboxing, and even logging your miles and routes online. Before leaving for your adventure, learn how to use a compass, and take the kids on a local orienteering course to test your skills. Let your tech-savvy child learn how to use GPS coordinates and find a compass or GPS app for your mobile device.

While you are on the trail, have fun while building those critical-thinking and problem-solving skills. Look no further than to what your child is learning in school to come up with fun conversational topics as you walk along.

+ Convert that math problem into an outdoor math problem: *If you have twenty-five trees and you cut down six, how many do you have left?*

+ Name categories of things: *Name three green (or any color) things along the trail. Name three animals that live in trees, three animals that make a noise, three animals that don't make noise.* Step this up a notch for the older child: *Name three carnivores that live in this habitat; name three edible plants found in this habitat.*

+ Engage children in I-spy activities (the five- to seven-year-olds will still enjoy these). You could focus on the sounds they are learning: *I spy something that begins with the letter L. That's right, leaf.*

+ Describe activities: *Name three words that describe bark. Name three words that describe the sky. Three words that describe the temperature.*

+ Play a sense game: *Close your eyes. What do you hear? What do you feel? Open your eyes. What do you see?*

+ Compare and contrast: *How are a pine tree and an oak tree the same and different?* Select random items within groups along the trail and continue this game.

- Ask leading questions about things like geology: *How old are the rocks?* This will probably lead to a discussion about dinosaurs and the Ice Age.

- Discuss life cycles of various animals, bugs, and plants.

- Discuss the seasons and what changes.

- Learn what various birds look and sound like. Use your binoculars to identify them.

- Do a tree-bark rubbing or a leaf rubbing. You will need paper and pencil or crayons. This makes an instant souvenir and conversation piece.

- Keep a journal. By first grade, most kids have acquired the skills to construct a simple story. Even the kindergartner is writing words, phrases, and drawing pictures. They can assemble their journal with pictures from the trip into a scrapbook when they get home. Let the techie child write on his tablet or iPad. This is a great keepsake to revisit a favorite hike.

If you are hiking in a national park, consider participating in the Junior Ranger program. This is an interactive program for school-age children, usually led by a ranger or naturalist, that will help your child learn more about the area your family is exploring. Kids really enjoy the recognition of earning a Junior Ranger badge. Ranger-led or naturalist-led hikes and programs are chock-full of interesting facts and knowledge that kids crave and adults discover they have forgotten. Even the adults will have fun learning about it again with their kiddos. Depending on the region or park that you are visiting, the program may vary, focusing on local animals, flora, or history. You and your children may learn about black bears in Shenandoah National Park, the importance of the bison to the Sioux in the Badlands, or the power of water in carving out the Grand Canyon. Once your child completes the program, she will be officially sworn in as a Junior Ranger, and depending on the park, she may receive a patch or certificate to commemorate the occasion.

Keep each other entertained while you are hiking or camping overnight:

+ Play animal charades. Do your best animal imitation and everyone has to guess what you are.

+ Tell stories to one another. Tell real ones and pretend stories.

+ Make up songs.

+ Turn on sky TV: At night, go out to a meadow or clearing and enjoy the stars.

+ Come up with your own trail name or work together to name each other. Long-distance hikers often acquire a fictitious name based on something that happened on their journey or a personal characteristic. What would your trail name be? Be nice. The names may stick! When I hiked the Appalachian Trail, I earned the trail name "Wrongfoot" after placing my insoles in the wrong boots and suffering from painful blisters.

Think Food, Think Water, Think Fun

Pack your kids' favorite snacks. Desirable food will help encourage your kids to eat and stay energized. Pack more food than you think you will need. Be sure to stop every fifteen or twenty minutes and have everyone take a drink. Refer to chapter 9 on food and water.

Your five-year-old will be twelve before you know it. The more adventures you take your kids on, the more opportunity you will have to spend quality time with one another, to build lasting memories, and to instill the value of hiking and the outdoors to your children.

HIKING AND CAMPING can bring extended family together in a fun, memorable way. Last summer, our nine-year-old nephew Dylan, my dad, and my stepmom joined us on our annual Shenandoah National Park (SNP) camping and hiking adventure in June. At the time, my daughter, Madison, was six, and my son, William, was a few weeks shy of his fourth birthday. My sister and her family live in Florida, over fifteen hours away from our home, so our kids don't have frequent opportunities to play or spend time with their cousins.

For three days we hiked, played in waterfalls, and sat around the campfire at night cooking s'mores and telling stories. William, Madison, and Dylan bonded over playing catch and Frisbee at the campsite. They had so much fun that when it came time for Dylan to leave, everyone was sad. The adventure was so enjoyable for Dylan, he recently called me to ask if we can take him on our summer adventure this year, too!

Planning extended-family gatherings at an outdoor vacation destination allows everyone to relax and enjoy one another. My extended family is spread across the United States, and we've started a Great Smoky Mountains National Park (GSMNP) Thanksgiving tradition. The GSMNP is a fun outdoor destination strategically located between my family in Florida and Ohio. To accommodate everyone's level of comfort, and in light of the cool fall weather, we rent a fully-furnished cabin in close proximity to the GSMNP. We take walks on the backcountry trails by day and break bread together at night. Last year, we watched my brother-in-law and nephew try their luck at trout fishing. It takes lots of practice and some local advice to catch a trout in the Smokies! For five days we hike together, eat together, play games together, and build lasting memories. Everyone has fun. I call it mountain medicine.

6

The Capstone Hiking Years

Reaching New Heights with Your Teenager:
Thirteen to Eighteen Years

Hiking with your teenager can be a fun and rewarding experience, or it could be a daunting challenge. If you introduced your child to hiking in the earlier years, you may stand a better chance of getting him out on a hike than a family who is just attempting such an endeavor now. Then again, many kids don't discover the fun of hiking in the great outdoors *until* their teenage years, and some teens will be reluctant to hit the trail with you regardless of their background. My point here is that no two teens or situations are the same. Teenagers have lots of new issues they didn't have in their early years—puberty, increased focus on their social life, boyfriends, girlfriends, peer pressure, college preparation, and sports, just to name a few. You need to take all these changes into consideration as you plan your hiking adventure.

With a few simple additions to your hiking plans, you may convince that reluctant kid to give hiking a try, and you may even cause your teenager to crave the next adventure. If you take your teen's wants and needs into consideration and make the adventure fun for him, you might just hook him into a healthy hobby that will endure a lifetime. If your kid refuses to willingly hike with you after you present your plan, you may need to throw in the towel for now. The one thing you don't want to do is push your child to do something they have no interest or desire to do. The harder you push, the further they might retreat. Keep in mind that he will grow through this stage and may have a change of heart in a few years.

Needs and Ability Assessment

Before presenting your adventure idea, take a good hard look at what your child's interests are. This will help you tailor your hiking plans to fit her current idea of "fun." Does your son or daughter spend lots of time with his or her friends? Then offer to let your child bring along a friend on the hike, with parental permission of course. This one gesture can be a huge game-changer, adding a social aspect—which may add miles, literally and figuratively—to your adventure. Is your teen physically active? Does she play sports? Is he in Scouts? Is she into sedentary hobbies (computer games, chess, TV)? When you present your plan to your teen, be sure your hiking adventure is within his or her physical capabilities. You want to set your child up for success. You also want to add a sense of adventure to your hike that perhaps your child didn't experience in his preteen years. This might involve a new destination or a longer hike. You want your teen to know that she is doing something more mature or at a higher skill level than what she did as a preteen. Be sure to include the latest hiking technology gadget to intrigue your tech-savvy teen. If your child is a seasoned hiker, be sure to give him or her more input in the hiking decisions and planning. Whatever your child's hobbies and interests are, by spending some time incorporating your teen's needs and abilities into your adventure, you are rigging your hike for success.

Pre-Trip Adventure Planning Party

Get everyone excited about the adventure. Before finalizing all the plans and arrangements, bring the hikers together. Assemble some general information about your destination. Order a pizza or whatever you need to do to create a fun trip-planning party atmosphere. You want your teen to know that he gets to help plan the adventure, or at least provide input. If you're hiking group will include your child's friends or hikers from outside your family, this is a great icebreaker to get to know everyone. Facilitate a conversation about where your hike will take you. Be sure to highlight all the cool sites, views, and activities you think the kids will enjoy. Gather around the computer and let the technology-savvy teen search the Internet for information about the destination. Be honest and realistic with everyone about the distance you plan to cover.

If your group wants to be involved with planning the

trip, outline and delegate some of the planning duties. You could have your computer-savvy child research the climate, terrain, and animals you may encounter—all of which will help you choose what gear to take and what to prepare for. If you have a seasoned Scout or outdoorsman in the group and he or she can read maps, have him or her come up with a few hiking routes and share them with the group. If you order any guidebooks or maps, have them sent to the teen who is helping to plan that aspect of the adventure.

The more your group becomes involved in the trip preparation, the higher the level of enthusiasm for the adventure. Regroup for another planning party and assemble the information you've gathered. Does your group have the skills and equipment for the hike? Attend local talks or slide shows about hiking adventures. Borrow DVDs from the library about the area in which you plan to hike and watch them together. Does anyone in your group have Wilderness First Aid certification? Sign up for a course with your local Red Cross. Are you or someone in your group able to read a map and use a compass or handheld GPS? Sign the group up for a local orienteering course. Are you hiking in bear or mountain-lion country? Study up on best practices for hiking in the animal habitat you will be in and share this information with the group. Will you ford mountain streams? These topics are covered in more detail in chapter 11. Add these scenarios to your shakedown hikes.

Gear Check and Train!

As mentioned in previous chapters, be sure everyone is outfitted in comfortable-fitting footwear and synthetic (no cotton!) socks. Your teenager is still growing, so buying expensive, name-brand non-cotton hiking clothing may not be the most practical purchase, unless you can hand the garments down to a sibling. If your teen is into the latest clothing fashions, you may need to make an exception or two and splurge for that name-brand fleece jacket to prevent mutiny. Make sure everyone has a properly fitted backpack and all the necessary gear for the terrain and climate you plan to traverse. Bring the group together to shop for the equipment and gear. This can be a fun pre-adventure outing. See chapter 12 on footwear, clothing, and gear for more information.

Several weeks before your adventure, plan a shakedown hike in a nearby park. Keep it fun and practical. Practice what to do for various scenarios such as a bear encounter or fording a stream. This may create some group humor and silliness, but take it seriously—this practice will prepare everyone for a real animal encounter or fording a fast-moving stream safely. Hike the actual distance you plan to walk during your adventure. Did everyone make it? If not, you may need to click back the miles you plan to cover or train more. Assess the morale of the group. Did everyone have fun? If not, why? Although this is serious training, you want to create a positive, fun atmosphere about the adventure. This training will help create excitement, develop some camaraderie, and weed out any bugs with gear. Treat everyone to ice cream or a special treat after the training hike to end on a celebratory note.

Before leaving town for your adventure, have everyone unpack their gear. Is anyone carrying unnecessary equipment? Do you have duplicate items in the group? For example, if you need only one or two water filters, it doesn't make sense to bring four. Does anyone have any last-minute gear issues? If your shoes or boots are causing friction now, that means you will get a blister on the trail. Eliminate the unnecessary equipment and return ill-fitting items for properly fitted gear. This last-minute check-in will save your group from potential misery on the hike.

Keep It Fun on the Trail

In order to keep each hiker engaged and interested during your hike, be sure to keep individual needs in mind on the trail. Even on a group hike, the adventure can be adapted to suit everyone's pace, interests, and ability. The more flexible you are on the trail, the more fun each hiker will have.

If you have some hikers in your group that are more athletically inclined than others and that have the necessary outdoor competency skills, let them blaze ahead of the group. Set some parameters such as waiting for the rest of the group at an agreed-upon point, prohibiting off-trail exploring, and staying with another hiking partner (the buddy system). Be mindful of potential dangers when allowing this: Are you in grizzly-bear country? Are there dangerous rivers to ford? Give leeway with safety in mind.

Make eating and drinking fun for all ages. Stop frequently and encourage everyone to take a drink of water to stay hydrated. Let the kids bring their favorite snacks. This will encourage them to eat and stay energized. You want your teen to eat nutritiously, but keep in mind that you would much rather have your teen walking and eating a candy bar then sitting home on the couch, chowing down on potato chips. If you're day hiking, you have much more flexibility with food—you can plan some elaborate feasts around a campfire at the end of the day. But if you are backpacking, you will need to plan your meals meticulously to avoid weighing down your pack. See chapter 9 on food for additional advice.

Let the teens pick the sites they want to visit and the activities they want to do along the trail. They may have no interest in viewing the peregrine falcon nest you want to see, but they would rather explore the cave behind the waterfall. Perhaps they want to take an extra-long lunch break and talk. Go with the interest and energy of the group and put your own interests on the back burner. You may discover that your teen has the same interest in history as you and wants to look for the derailed locomotive along the trail. The point is, if your teens pick the activity instead of you telling them what they're going to do, they will have the autonomy they crave and will enjoy the adventure more.

Including the latest gadgets related to hiking might make all the difference to your computer-savvy teenagers. Let's face it, unlike most middle-age adults, our kids have grown up in the computer age, with buds plugging their ears and their hands clutching the latest portable gaming system. Embrace your teen's technology habits and direct your kid's attention to the latest electronic hiking gear. As mentioned in previous chapters, hiking gear is loaded with gadgets like your new LED headlamp flashlight, a personal GPS tracking system, a satellite phone, a handheld GPS for navigation, a pedometer, a watch that monitors your pulse, a digital waterproof camera with GPS, solar-powered battery chargers, and so on. As a matter of fact, your teen might be able to teach *you* a few things about how to use these gadgets! This gear might intrigue even the most sedentary teen enough to put down his virtual game and give hiking a try. Your teen may come to realize that nothing on a screen, no matter how great the graphics, can replace the multidimensional outdoors.

Bringing technology onto the trail, however, requires some etiquette. In order to get your kids to come along, perhaps you allowed them to bring their MP3 player, a cell phone, or a tablet computer. You're just thrilled to get your kid onto the trail, plugged in or not. On the other hand, other hikers and campers are trying to escape the technological world and may not want to share camp with someone talking on a cell phone, typing on a computer, or playing music. Respect those around you. In your planning and preparation, lay down some ground rules with these devices. Walking down the trail while listening to music may impede your child's ability to hear that bear rustling in the bushes or that moose running down the trail and could lead to a dangerous encounter. Cell phones are extremely unreliable in the backcountry and should not be your only answer to an emergency. I suggest limiting leisure use of computer gadgets to areas away from other hikers and only for brief periods (for example, let the homesick teen call Mom or Dad on the cell but limit her to one call a day).

All this technology can lead to more adventurous fun even if the devices fail or the batteries go dead. If your group is properly prepared, someone has a good old-fashioned map and compass and knows how to use them. When those batteries go dead, challenge your teens to see if they can navigate without electronic assistance. Intrigue your group with a communication exercise. How could you communicate with the outside world if your cell phone doesn't work? (Answers: Use smoke signals, flares, whistles, or reflector mirrors, or send hikers to get help, depending on the situation.) It will not only be fun learning about survival, but it will also increase your child's level of confidence.

Group time is always fun. Gather everyone around a campfire or in a circle. Spark conversations about the highs and lows of the day. Keep a group journal. Note-taking duty would be a great assignment for the teen who brought his iPad. Perhaps you have an artist or someone into scrap-booking who could assemble all the photos and group journal into a trip album.

Many of the same preteen hiking activities can be fun for your teenager as well. Just step the task up a notch. Build on your child's critical-thinking skills. Go around the group and ask questions such as, *How is hiking metaphorically like life? If you could take only one item into the woods, what would it be and why?* Assigning trail names is a fun activity across all ages. Your group may enjoy trail songs, charades, night hikes, or sky TV (star gazing). Some of your teens may enjoy ranger- and naturalist-led talks or hikes. Remember, although you may need to provide many options or sugges-tions, as long as you let your teen decide which activity she wants to do, she will have fun.

The teen years are the capstone years of youth. Even if your group includes your child's friends or your neighbors, your adventure will still allow you to impress a life lesson or two, just by being a caring parent who took the time to lead your child on a survival adventure before he or she strikes out into the world. Hiking and backpacking can help teens learn about the important, simple things in life. Many teenagers are into tangible items. They may want the latest fashionable clothing or that new video game, but when they have to carry everything on their back, they learn a quick lesson on what one really needs. Regardless of how old your kid is, he will always be your baby, even after he turns eighteen. Your adventure has hopefully given your child a natural, healthy hobby to escape from the hustle and bustle of domestic life as he grows older and navigates "his world." That child who refused to go hiking with you just may have a change of heart and take you on an adventure one day! Perhaps that hike you took with her in the preteen years planted the seed for future hiking endeavors.

AS CHILDREN GROWING up in the seventies and eighties, my friends and I had more freedom than we allow our kids today. It was a simpler time. Perhaps our parents were a little naive or, without our modern twenty-four-hour news cycle, they weren't as informed of all the bad things that could happen or go wrong from letting their children roam freely. Most parents today would not consider letting their kids play outside without supervision. Outdoor wilderness opportunities were more abundant for most kids back then. My neighborhood was surrounded by undeveloped forest, where I would escape and climb trees, establish forts, and play hide-and-seek. I could run and play on my grandfather's sprawling hundred-acre farm for hours. That farm is no more and the forest surrounding the neighborhood where I grew up is now a subdivision.

My first "real" hike didn't occur until my teenage years, and it was so profound that it inspired me to walk the entire Appalachian Trail later in life. I stepped onto the Appalachian Trail for the first time as a fourteen-year-old kid on summer vacation with my family in the Great Smoky Mountains National Park (GSMNP). I had never been to the park before, nor had I ever gone on an overnight hike. My family and I set up camp at one of the national park campgrounds, Elkmont, at the foot of Clingmans Dome. At 6,643 feet, it is the highest mountain in the Smokies. My two brothers and I decided to hike up the mountain, leaving behind our parents, a cooler full of food, and a comfortable camper. Obviously we weren't thinking clearly, nor were we properly trained. We didn't have the proper backcountry gear essential to hiking, so we headed up with our sleeping bags in trashcan liners along with some candy bars, canned food, and two-liter pop bottles filled with water.

We intended to stay in the Double Spring Gap Shelter along the Appalachian Trail, a makeshift shanty for overnight hikers located only a short distance from the summit. Halfway up the mountain, the three of us lay down along the trail, not wanting to go a step farther. A ranger came hiking down the trail from the summit and advised us to get off our duffs and scramble up the mountain if we wanted to make it to the shelter by nightfall. We all stood up and began hiking as fast as we could in fear of being exposed to the bear-infested forest without light or shelter. That ranger gave us the firecracker—the motivation—we needed, and we finally arrived at the shelter at dusk. The hike was the toughest thing I had ever done physically, and I still felt it in my muscles a week later. I was never so happy to be back with our parents and a cooler full of food the next day. We learned to appreciate all of the simple luxuries of life after just two days in the woods.

Of course, we didn't appreciate the historical significance of the Appalachian Trail on that first hike. We were just proud of our physical accomplishment and the bravery that carried us through the bear- and snake-infested wilderness. We were thankful to be alive. We didn't realize that we had spent the night in a shelter along one of the oldest, longest footpaths in North America. Years passed before I went on a hike again. In college, I acquired some basic hiking equipment and returned to the Great Smoky Mountains for a hiking adventure. I was in better shape than during my teenage encounter with hiking, and I had appropriate gear this time. I actually began to enjoy the rigorous endurance required for backpacking. Throughout college, I hiked frequently during school vacations and led several college groups on weeklong hikes in the Great Smoky Mountains.

The GSMNP became my mountain playground. If I wasn't visiting family during college breaks, I was hiking somewhere in the Smokies. The world has changed, and letting your teenager roam unsupervised may be out of the question for you, but never doubt the power of allowing your teen to pursue their own outdoor adventure.

7

Everyone Has a Place on the Trail

Including the Hiker with Special Needs

scaping to the great outdoors offers children with special needs a world of opportunity to de-stress, relax, learn, and have fun. The same reasons that you enjoy hiking and being in the outdoors apply to children with special needs as well. The term *children with special needs* broadly includes children that don't have all the functionality of a normally developing child. It encompasses children who have conditions ranging from mild to severe that necessitate varying degrees of help from others for taking care of their daily needs. Whether you have a child who uses a wheelchair; can't speak; or has cognitive disabilities, autism, severe allergies, or blindness, or other issues, taking him or her on a hike can still be a grand adventure. Every year, many families with children who have special needs tackle the great outdoors, and so can you. You may just have to modify your hiking adventure to fit your child's abilities. The key to a successful hiking adventure with a child who has special needs is being flexible. The outdoors offers a natural, healthy element as an extension to the child's environment and is worth the extra effort to get your kid outdoors in a fun and safe manner.

Preparation and Research

Planning a hike with a child who has special needs adds an element of adventure even before you hit the trail. You will tap into some of the same problem-solving skills you will use on the hike itself, while you navigate how to accommodate your special circumstance. Each child and situation is unique and will require some additional extra steps when planning your adventure. The more severe the special need, the more preparation will be required. If you already travel with your child, you most likely already have a process in place to accommodate your child's specific condition (for example, EpiPen and Benadryl for your child's peanut allergy, a wheelchair access checklist, calming methods for a child made anxious by environmental changes, and so forth). You may just have to tweak your process to include a hiking contingency. You will become more refined with each trip you take. Due to the wide array of conditions and disorders, there is no specific method of preparing for an adventure. This is something you will have to determine within your own set of circumstances. You may need to seek advice from professionals familiar with your child: pediatrician, physical therapist, occupational therapist, speech-language therapist, special educator, teacher, support group, allergist, and so on. Do you know anyone with a similar circumstance who has hiked with his or her child with special needs? Such a person may be a great resource for ideas and strategies, and you might even get some hand-me-down equipment.

With just a few modifications, your hike may be very similar to hiking with a child without special needs, or you may have to go about your approach in an entirely different manner, depending on your child's condition. For example: If you're dealing with a life-threatening peanut allergy, you can probably hike anywhere a typical child can go. You will just need to make sure you have the child's EpiPen and Benadryl and a medical emergency plan, which you should have for any trip. Hiking with a child who is in a wheelchair, however, will require refining your hike plan to include wheelchair-accessible trails. You may be able to carry your physically disabled child in the same equipment as one would with typically developing children (infant carrier and child carrier) until your child reaches the maximum weight recommendations for each carrier or becomes too heavy for you to carry. This is a decision that you will need to make based on the conditions affecting your child and in consultation with the health professionals who know your circumstances. All the national parks, and most state and local parks, have wheelchair-accessible trails.

As with all hike preparation with children, before making hiking travel plans, try a short hike outing in your local park. This will give you a simulated idea of what it will be like at your destination. Even in normal circumstances it is recommended that you acquire the proper gear and train before heading out of town to your hiking destination. A child with special needs may require extra pre training efforts. Depending on the severity of your child's condition, you may need to plan a destination based on your child's abilities and medical condition. If you've never hiked or camped with your child and you are unsure of what he or she is capable, think about all the outings you have taken: a walk around the neighborhood, a trip to the zoo, a visit with friends or relatives, a walk in the local park. What equipment and gear did you need for each of those events that made it fun and comfortable for your child? Make a list of those items. How long can your child comfortably travel in a vehicle? Has he ever flown before? How did the flight go with your child? Does he like the outdoors? Take your child to a local park and give it a try. Did your child enjoy the hike? What aspect of the event did he enjoy the most? Were there any issues or frustrating moments? On your hike, did your child enjoy the shaded woods, open fields, or the streams and lakes? What activity does he enjoy—fishing, riding in a boat, sitting under a tree, walking? All of this information will help you select a destination that will fit the needs of your child. Research parks that have plenty of the outdoor aspect your child enjoys. If traveling long distances in a vehicle is difficult, what hiking destinations are within a reasonable drive? You'd be surprised at just how many hiking opportunities are within a short ride of most large- and medium-size cities. If flying is an option, that may be the best method of travel to get within a reasonable drive of your out-of-town hiking destination. The key is to make the event as fun and stress-free as possible.

A camping trip can help fill the outdoor experience for children with special needs, especially children who are fully dependent on you for all their daily needs. Many of the aspects of nature you enjoy on a hike can be experienced in a campground. Parks have gone to great lengths to enhance the outdoor experience for park visitors with special needs. All national parks, state parks, and metro parks that offer camping have designated handicap campsites usually located near the bathhouse and restrooms. You can rent an RV or acquire a tent to accommodate all your extra equipment. If you need electricity for medical equipment (ventilator, breathing treatment, and so forth), you can select a park that has electrical hookups or that allows generators. The campgrounds are usually paved, making it easy to push a wheelchair around. If you have additional typically functioning children along for the trip, a campsite serves as a base camp where you can all come together around the campfire, at mealtime, and to play games. With additional adult help, all of the children can take day trips centered on their own abilities, with adaptation or not. Whether you plan separate outings or activities in which everyone can participate, the campsite brings everyone together in a natural way so no one feels left out, regardless of ability.

Depending on the severity of your child's condition, you may want to attend an adaptive outdoor pursuit camp. A few clicks of an Internet search will yield all sorts of adaptive outdoor pursuit camps and programs. Depending on your financial resources and location, you may gain a lifetime of confidence and knowledge on how to go about hiking with your child with special needs by attending one of these camps that matches your specific need. Many of these camps require or allow the caregiver to attend. You might gain all sorts of tips on how to assess and modify equipment specific to your child and hiking. This might be just the trick to give you the knowledge and confidence to assemble your own hiking adventures.

Horses and mules may help out with your hiker with special needs. Many backcountry trails in the western United States are graded for horse and mule access. Several companies offer horse pack services ranging from full backcountry accommodations (meals and a horse to ride) or simply delivering your gear to each of your planned campsites. Depending on your special need, this service might play a role—especially if you are looking for a way to experience the remote backcountry but cannot carry all the equipment necessary to do so.

Now that you've chosen your destination, it's time to acquire all the equipment you'll need. Refer to the chapters that best describe the age and functionality of your child. You may need to mix and match tips and lists depending on your child's physical size or cognitive ability. Refer to chapter 12 on equipment and clothing. It's important to make sure you have all the right equipment in advance so you can train with your child. If you plan to modify the equipment you acquire to retrofit it to your child's adaptive device (cutting a sleeve off a jacket, tearing the liner out of hiking pants, and so forth), you may want to buy used equipment or avoid name brands to keep your costs down. After you discover the gear that works best and hiking becomes a regular mainstay in your routine, then you can invest in higher-quality gear, knowing you will reap the benefits.

Social Stories may help prepare a child who has difficulty adjusting to new environments and settings. A Social Story is a common technique used with autistic children to prepare them for a transition to an activity or new environment. A picture schedule that sequences the steps involved in hiking can be useful for any young child to prepare him or her for your adventure. For the higher-functioning older child, you could write a Social Story (a written description of the activity you are about to embark on) explaining proper etiquette during the hike. You can write about what you might see. You can talk about how you will stop for water breaks and your child's favorite snacks along the way. You can show pictures of the park you will be hiking in. Demonstrate what the trail markers look like. Log on to the park's website and share the descriptions and park photos with your kids.

Safety Concerns

Whenever we head into the outdoors, we expose ourselves to the elements, the sun, and bugs. A child with special needs might not let you know she is getting sunburned or that a tick is on her leg. She won't know she's dehydrated. Stop frequently for sips of water. You will need to take extra care to be sure you've lathered your child up with plenty of pediatrician-recommended sunscreen. Be sure your child isn't sitting in the direct sunlight. If your child allows, fit her with a wide-brimmed hat and sunglasses. Be sure to apply age-recommended bug repellent. Check her for ticks and bug bites each day. See chapter 10 for information about bugs and sun. If your child is going to be hiking with you or out in the elements, follow the clothing and equipment recommendations in chapter 12. Check your child frequently for early signs of hypothermia or heat exhaustion. It's recommended to always hike with an additional companion. I recommend hiking with at least two adults when hitting the trails with children. A simple incident within reach of domestic amenities can become very complex without those resources in the backcountry. Never hike alone.

If you are worried about your child running off or if she doesn't have a good sense of safety, avoid hiking near dangerous areas like cliff edges, raging streams, and rock scrambles. If your child is verbal or can make a vocal sound, can you teach her to verbally respond to a stranger calling out her name or to blow a whistle if she gets lost? These skills could be lifesaving if you become separated or your child gets lost. Having a procedure in place is half the battle. The sound of a whistle can travel much farther than a voice calling for help. Three whistle bursts is the universal distress sound. You can also place a GPS tracking system on your child if you are concerned she might get lost. There is a product available by Optimal Tracking (www.optimaltracking.com/en) made specifically for this purpose.

Keep the Hiking or Camping Adventure Fun!

Now that you have identified what your child is capable of doing, let the fun begin! Whether your child is in a wheelchair or walking alongside you, she will get something out of the adventure that only the outdoors can provide. You just might have to facilitate the experience. Many of the fun ideas shared in previous chapters can be applied to your child with special needs. A child with significant needs may require hands-on facilitation to maximize her outdoor experience.

Facilitate the Outdoor Sensory Experience

"Hiking fills our senses with enjoyable pleasures," says pediatric and school-based occupational therapist Kay **Pfeifer**, from Cincinnati, Ohio. **Pfeifer** continues: "These pleasures can involve auditory-sound, tactile, taste, smell, visual, and movement." You can really enhance your adventure through sensory exploration. Explore all your child's senses in the outdoors. Place a leaf in his hands and gently guide his other hand over the leaf to feel the texture. You can do this with bark, rocks, and anything within reason. Talk about how the items feel: rough, smooth, hard, soft, and so on. **Pfeifer** recommends seeking out all the sounds of the hike—sticks and leaves crunching under your feet, birds chirping, branches and leaves blowing in the wind, and animal movements. Preview various species of bird sounds you might encounter before you head out at www.allaboutbirds.org. While you're exploring, record the sounds you hear on your phone or with a tape recorder.

Pfeifer recommends capturing all the beautiful sites with a camera. If possible, let your child take the pictures. Zoom in on various textures of trees and rocks. Point out the differences between the textures. Make a booklet when you get home of all the awesome pictures you took for your child to enjoy long after your trip.

Pfeifer suggests exploring your child's sense of touch by selecting items along your hike to feel: bark, rocks, shells, and the like. Before heading to the woods, make a sensory bracelet using packing tape or duct tape with the sticky side out. Stick items of various textures onto the bracelet. As you hike along, try to find items that match the various textures on your bracelet. Remember to leave everything in the woods and take nothing but memories and pictures. Let your child carry a fidget item if he seeks one out. This could be a hiking stick or perhaps something from home. Encourage your child to explore items by picking them up, being mindful of poison ivy and other potentially harmful items. Splash in the creek. Rock hopping across the creek increases the child's motor planning and problem-solving skills.

Pfeifer emphasizes the importance that children receive sensory stimulation for optimal development. All children—verbal or nonverbal, mobile or nonambulatory, sensory-seeker or non-sensory-seeker—will benefit from exposure to the outdoors, whether you're hiking down a footpath, rolling on a boardwalk along the beach, or splashing in a creek. Start with a short trip close to home. A brief thirty minutes may be enough to give your child a fun new adventure. Stop your adventure while your kid is having fun, before fatigue gets in the way. This will give your child a positive memory and increase her interest in hiking again.

MY BROTHER, AARON, was born with cerebral palsy and severe cognitive deficits. He is the inspiration behind my Appalachian Trail book, *A Walk for Sunshine*. Aaron is nonverbal; he doesn't walk and is reliant on others for all his daily needs. Aaron now resides in a residential home, but when we were kids, we took Aaron camping. We pushed his wheelchair on walks around the paved campground paths. Aaron continues to enjoy the outdoors. Aaron's home, Sunshine, is nestled along a creek bed with a wheelchair-accessible boardwalk. He enjoys being pushed into the forest along the boardwalk. He will sit quietly and seems to enjoy listening to the birds chirping. Aaron also enjoys fishing with our dad. Dad is quite the fisherman, and he has taken Aaron along. This requires the help of Sunshine staff and a special dock to lock his wheels in place. Aaron joins us each year for an annual five-kilometer charity walk for Sunshine. He rolls along with us, as family and friends take turns pushing his chair. Aaron always seems at ease outside in the fresh air with family. Aaron's most powerful mode of communicating from his limited nonverbal world is through gestures and facial expressions. His smile assures all of us that he is happy in the great outdoors.

8

See You in a Few Days!

Backpacking with Kids

Backpacking with your child can be a life-changing experience. Stepping away from your vehicle and disappearing down the trail overnight, and carrying everything to survive on your back, creates an element of adventure like no other. You are relying on the contents of your pack and your survival knowledge. No hot showers, no refrigerators, no TV—just you, your kids, the earth, and the sky. A backpacking adventure puts the entertainment and fun in your hands. Even just one night in the woods is sure to result in some spectacular memories.

When your child is seven or eight years old, he should be of the weight and ability to physically carry some of his own gear without injury. Prior to this age, you are better off setting up a base camp and day hiking. The mantra of hiking is "The lighter the pack, the more enjoyable the journey." If your child can't carry his own gear, you will have to shoulder everything. It can be done, and quite a few families backpack with their youngsters, but unless you are conditioned to carry heavy loads, you could injure yourself. The burdensome load can also suck all the fun out of the journey and distract your mind from the special time on the trail with your kids. If you are insistent on backpacking overnight with a child who is not ready to shoulder his own load, you have several options. Some parks have graded trails allowing for horse, mules, and llamas to carry equipment. You might be able to hire a Sherpa to portage your gear, or you could research trails that offer hostels and lodging along the way to eliminate the need to carry a tent, sleeping bags, a stove, and meals. Of course, the added logistical requirements of lodging, a Sherpa, or four-legged caravans will require additional planning. The requirements will also limit you to a smaller array of travel destinations and hit your pocketbook. So, for the purpose of keeping your backpacking experience simple, practical, and affordable, you are better off waiting until your child is of the age and ability to carry his own gear in his backpack. It's much easier to stay at car-accessible base camps or lodging that allows you to day hike pretty much anywhere with your child without feeling like a Sherpa.

A child should not carry more than ten to twenty percent of his or her body weight. A seven- or eight-year-old child can hoist eleven to fifteen pounds on her back, and if done right, this will not result in injury. For example, a seven-year-old boy weighing fifty-five pounds can carry a maximum of eleven pounds. That is approximately equivalent to the weight of a sleeping bag, water, a fleece jacket, a rain parka, and regular clothing. A great website to help you calculate your gear is www.weighmygear.com. Be sure to include the weight of the pack in your calculations. Packs weigh several pounds, even when empty. At this young age, your child will still need you to carry some of his extra weight (food, tent, accessories). Hiking with several adults or older kids will allow you to distribute the extra supplies.

Preparation

Overnight hiking requires preparation beyond planning for a day hike. You will need more gear: a stove, a pot, spoons, a sleeping pad, a sleeping bag, a change of clothes, and more food than you need for a day hike. You will also need a larger pack to accommodate all of the additional gear (refer to chapters 9 and 12 on food and packs). If you've never backpacked before, educate yourself on the basics. Attend a backpacking clinic at your local outfitter or university, read up on backpacking basics, and rent some DVDs on backpacking from your local library. Consult with experienced hikers, and if possible, go on an overnight with an experienced backpacker.

Just as you did for your day hike, you will need to fit your child properly into a pack for overnight hiking and camping. There are many factors that go into a backpack decision, and your needs are best met by visiting an outfitter that specializes in backpacking supplies. There are independent outfitters, regional outfitters like Blue Ridge Mountain Sports, and national outfitters such as Recreation Equipment Incorporated (REI) and Eastern Mountain Sports (EMS), all of which will be able to accommodate your backpacking supply needs. There are plenty of other options, such as online retailers, but certain items like backpacks and footwear are best bought in person to ensure a proper fitting. You might want to rent your gear from a local university or outfitter before you make an expensive backpack or tent purchase so you can become familiar with what works best for you and your kids.

Bring your kids to the outfitter with you to fit into a pack and acquire trail shoes. A pack-fitting specialist will measure your child's torso and hip size. They will inquire about your needs, such as the size of the pack (cubic inches or liters) and internal or external frame. Internal frames conform to your body and are good for rugged trails requiring free range of movement. External frame packs are designed for heavier loads but lack the free movement agility of the internal frame. This is a personal choice. If you are selecting a pack for your child, try to find one that offers room to grow. Most packs easily adjust to different sizes and shapes. The pack specialist will load the pack with the approximate weight of what your child should carry. Make sure the pack fits correctly on your child. After all the straps (hip belt, shoulder straps, load lifter straps, sternum straps, and stabilizer straps) are tightened, does the weight of the pack rest on her hips? Is the shoulder strap snug over her shoulders? Can she walk with the pack? Ask your child how it feels.

Hiking-grade footwear is paramount when carrying a heavier backpack than the one you use for day hiking. Your child can get away with a comfortable pair of sneakers or trail shoes when carrying a smaller day pack, but now that she has an added load on her back, you want to be sure she's wearing a sturdy boot or shoe with a hard, trail-tough sole to prevent injury. Have your child measured for footwear. Be sure your child is wearing her hiking socks when she tries on the footwear.

After you acquire your gear, you need to practice carrying all your equipment. Better yet, you should do a shakedown hike with all your gear to make sure everything works. This could be as simple as hiking through the neighborhood and camping in the backyard for the night, or hiking overnight to a nearby destination. The idea is to make sure everything fits, the stove works, the water filter pumps, the meals you're planning to cook please everyone's palate, and everyone is comfortably able to carry their gear. This is the best time to discover any gear issues—before you reach your hiking destination. If you have any issues with your equipment, it's much easier to make adjustments or return and exchange gear while you're in town and near the retailer. Nothing is more stressful than having to cancel your trip or return earlier than planned because a stove didn't work, your pack is causing you pain, or the boots are giving you blisters.

There are several other items you will need beyond the backpack and footwear. Even if you don't use trekking poles when day hiking, you may find with the added weight of a backpack that the poles spread out the work to your upper body and give you added stability. Trekking poles take practice, and kids will need some special instruction on how to use them. Never let your children run with the poles. Demonstrate how to use the poles and walk alongside your child. All the additional hiking items and tips beyond the pack and footwear (food, water, first aid, and so forth) will be discussed in the following chapters. An entire gear inventory list for an overnight hike can be found in the age-appropriate appendix.

As you plan your overnight camp or shelter destinations, be conservative in the distance you plan to travel each day. It's better to err toward underachieving to keep morale high. You want everyone to feel successful. The first few overnight hikes will be a time of discovery. Remember, you want to build positive memories with your kids so they will want to backpack again and again. Leading them on a grueling march into the wee hours of evening is a sure way to end the positive experience for the beginning backpacker. Stop midday or early afternoon and set up camp. This will give your kids a chance to play, gather firewood, and enjoy the destination. Save the rigorous, high-mileage hike for that athletic high school child seeking an endurance challenge.

Many of the same fun activities mentioned in the day hiking chapters apply for overnight hikers as well. For example, if you are hiking with a seven-year-old, refer to chapter 5 on hiking with the school-age hiker. If you're hiking with an adolescent, refer to chapter 6.

WHEN MY DAUGHTER, Madison, was seven and my son, William, was almost five, we decided they were ready for their first overnight hike. After all, they had been hiking with us since they were infants, and Madison's weight and ability allowed for her to safely carry some of her gear: a sleeping bag, her clothing, her water, a book, and some interactive hiking toys (binoculars, a multipurpose survival tool, and the like). William was able to shoulder his clothes and water in a children's day pack. The rest of the kids' gear would have to be carried by my wife and me. We made plans for a two-day hike along the Appalachian Trail (AT). Our kids had been fascinated with the AT after hearing my stories about my Georgia to Maine thru-hike, and they were eager to go. This would also allow us to utilize the shelters along the trail (three-walled, roof-covered shanties) and eliminate the weight of a tent to compensate for the added gear Beth and I were shouldering. We made shelter reservations along the AT, in the Shenandoah National Park. Prior to our trip, we outfitted the kids in packs and trail shoes and took a few shakedown hikes in local parks. The kids wanted to use hiking poles just like me, so we included trekking poles in our training hikes.

We began our AT hike at Big Meadows Campground, in the Shenandoah National Park. Our destination was Rock Spring Hut, three and a half miles north along the AT. William took the lead to set the pace. We stopped every fifteen minutes to sip our water, and we stopped for a trail snack after about an hour. Madison wanted to take a turn as the lead hiker, but her pace was much faster than William's, so William and I let Madison and Beth get a head start. This way, William wouldn't feel pressured to keep up. We arrived at the shelter by late afternoon, allowing plenty of daylight to set up camp, cook dinner, and let the kids play. Four AT thru-hikers, who had hiked all the way from Georgia and were heading to Maine, were already set up for the night. They welcomed us and scooted their gear over, allowing all four of us space to roll out our sleeping bags. The kids hiked down the mountain with me to pump water from a spring.

Filtering water was a big hit. I never thought fetching water would be so fun. The kids felt like they were helping out and being useful. We let William and Madison choose the dinner entrée before we left on the adventure to ensure that they would eat a lot. So, macaroni and cheese it was, with a side of baby carrots. After dinner, Madison pulled out her special dessert—s'mores. As we were packing for the trip, I explained to her that the graham crackers might crumble in our packs. She left the room and returned with an empty oatmeal canister to transport them. What a smart little girl! We packed the graham crackers in a plastic baggy, placed them in the container, placed chocolate bars inside, and stuffed a small bag of marshmallows on top. As Madison unpacked the s'mores ingredients from the container, smiling, pleased that the graham crackers arrived uncracked and proud of her canister solution, something else was going on. The thru-hikers were eyeing the s'mores ingredients, hoping to get an invitation to join us for dessert. In anticipation of this, I had packed along plenty of extras. The kids roasted marshmallows over a blazing fire stoked by the AT hikers. In assembly-line fashion, we sandwiched the chocolate and marshmallows between the graham crackers and handed each hiker a treat. As the sun set, we hung our food up on a bear pole and the kids changed into their nighttime outfits. They zipped into their sleeping bags and read books with their headlamps. One thru-hiker pulled out a ukulele and played a few tunes. The kids felt like thru-hikers themselves. What a neat opportunity for them to sleep in a shelter and interact with these long-distance hikers while they were on a journey of a lifetime! After dark, several more thru-hikers arrived, filling the shelter to capacity, and soon others pitched tents nearby. Madison was so excited with the adventure that she had a hard time falling asleep. It stormed throughout the night, and in the morning the sky was clear blue. After a granola bar breakfast, we packed up, said good-bye to our bunkmates and wished them luck on their journey to Maine, and headed down the trail back to Big Meadows Campground.

Our kids' first backpacking trip was a success. My goal was to introduce overnight hiking in such a way that Madison and William would enjoy it so much that they would want to do it again. As we neared the end of the trail, I asked the kids what they thought of our adventure. Madison responded, "Daddy, this was so fun! I want to hike the whole AT when I turn ten." William piped in, saying, "I like being outside all the time and sleeping in a shelter next to my family." A short while later, we arrived at our base camp and headed up to the Wayside store for lunch and the ice-cream treat we promised the kids at the end of the hike. As we sat there enjoying the blackberry ice cream, I was relishing something bigger. My kids had been hiking with us since they were infants, using all the tips and techniques mentioned in this book, and it had paid off. It was official—our kids loved hiking and backpacking. Yahoo!

9

Think Food! Think Water! Think Fun!

Tips and Menus for Drinking and Dining Out, Literally, on the Trail

Water

Hydration is critical on a hike. An average adult should consume at least two quarts of water a day, and a child's consumption will vary based on size, age, and exertion. This doesn't apply to young infants relying on breast milk or formula. The key to helping your kids stay hydrated is to make it fun. Hydration hose systems, like the CamelBak or Platypus, encourage kids to drink more frequently because the sipping hose is near their mouths for easy access. Colorful hard plastic or aluminum bottles, like a Nalgene bottle, are great for carrying water on a hike because you can put any liquid in them without the bottle retaining the taste or odor. Be sure that your water system is free of BPA (Bisphenol A), because plastics containing BPA are suspected to cause cancer. Most products clearly state on the packaging whether they are BPA-free.

Does your child routinely drink water at home? What are her favorite liquids to drink? If she already freely consumes water, this will be an easy transition to hiking. If your child prefers milk, juice, or other beverages, then you may need to bring along some drink mix to whip up her favorite beverage to encourage hydration. Kids who are reluctant to sip their water might be swayed with some lemonade or Gatorade. You can even whip up some powdered milk. Stop for drink breaks every fifteen or twenty minutes, especially in warm weather.

You should have a water resupply plan before you hit the trail. Research water availability and sources along your route. Consider the weather and environmental conditions of the area. Some springs dry up in late summer or may be dry if the area is experiencing drought conditions. Check on water availability with sources familiar with the area, such as the park staff or trail organizations.

If you plan to be on the trail more than a few hours, you should bring along a method to treat water taken from lakes, streams, springs, and ponds along the trail. Treat all water before consumption even if it looks clean, unless the source is listed as safe for consumption in your trail guide or on your map. The primary concern when hiking in the United States is *Giardia lamblia* (giardia) and *Cryptosporidium* (known as "crypto"), both of which inhabit water contaminated from animal and human feces. Both are protozoa and will cause diarrhea and other unpleasant gastrointestinal issues. If you contract giardia or crypto, you may require medical intervention. You can also contract other bacteria and virus-borne pathogens from untreated water sources, especially in developing countries. I've listed several methods below to treat your water. Spend some time at your local outfitter. Talk with a knowledgeable staff member about the pros and cons of each water-treatment method. After you acquire a water-treatment system, try it out at home before you hit the trail. Become comfortable with all the features. Have a backup plan or secondary treatment source if your system malfunctions.

Water pump filtration systems work well for both day hiking and overnight backpacking. Your water will still be cold from the source you retrieved it from, and it is ready to drink immediately after filtering. Research your filter purchase. Be sure that your filter is "absolute 1 micron" or smaller, which is proven effective in preventing giardia and crypto. Filters with "absolute 0.3 microns" or smaller are also effective against bacteria. A good filter system will protect you from the two main contamination issues with water in the backcountry, but you are still vulnerable to other water borne viruses with these systems.

Chemically treating your water with iodine or chlorine dioxide tablets is another method. Iodine and chlorine di-oxide are effective in treating water for bacteria and viruses. Be aware that iodine is ineffective against crypto. Chlorine dioxide tablets aren't the most reliable in removing crypto, either. If you combine a water-pump filter with your chem-ical treatment, you can effectively treat your water from bacteria, protozoa, and viruses. Some pump filters have chemical treatment added to the filtration. The CDC warns against the use of iodine if you are pregnant.

UV water treatment systems have grown in popularity

recently due to their proven effectiveness in treating water for bacteria, protozoa, and viruses. UV water treatment systems are lightweight, and they treat the water quickly and leave no aftertaste. Long-distance hikers are beginning to use this method more and more. You will need batteries, so be sure to bring along some spares.

Boiling your water is the most effective way to kill all water borne pathogens, but carrying a stove on a day hike isn't all that practical, and unpacking a stove midday is time-consuming. If you are backpacking overnight, then boiling water makes sense at breakfast or dinner. You can make a cup of coffee, and your kids may enjoy a cup of hot cocoa in the morning.

Food

Don't forget to pack your child's favorite snacks and meals. Desirable food will help encourage your child to eat and stay energized. If your child knows you brought along his favorite munchies, stopping for a snack or lunch on the trail will be a big hit. Introducing new foods to your child on a hike is a gamble and may not go over so well. Try out your hiking meals at home first, and see if everyone likes them. Day hikes are easy to pack for. You simply pack a picnic lunch along with some high-energy snacks. Bring extra snacks, packing more food than you think you will need. If you get caught out on the trail longer than you anticipated, the extra food will serve you well. Don't be afraid of candy on the trail, either. Your child will burn off the extra calories from that chocolate bar, and they might surprise you with a burst of energy when they need it most. No two kids are the same, so you will need to come up with your own food lists that match your child's tastes. Below is a list of lunch foods and snacks that my children love on the trail. It will help get you started.

Day Hiking Snacks and Lunch Ideas

* peanut butter and jelly bagels (bagels won't crumble like bread will in your pack)

* tortilla ham and cheese wraps

* Oscar Mayer Lunchables

* string cheese

* mini carrots

* grapes

* bananas

* Zbars by Clif

* Sharkies organic energy fruit chews

* Fruit Roll-Ups

* Goldfish and other crackers

* granola bars

* breakfast fruit bars

* trail mix (cereal with raisins and M&M'S)

* Sausage, cheese, and crackers

If you're planning to backpack overnight, you will need to plan breakfast, lunch, dinner, and snacks for each day. Several of the day-hiking lunch items mentioned above will work for backpacking, with the exception of the bulky fresh fruit and anything that requires refrigeration. Try out your food and your stove at home before your trip to make sure everything works and you can cook food the kids will enjoy. When planning your meals and snacks, think compact, lightweight, and filling. An adult hiker needs an average of two pounds of food per day, and children's portions will vary. Bring items that are easy to prepare or ready to eat. Select foods that need just a little bit of water to prepare. You can buy some pretty tasty freeze-dried backpacking food for breakfasts and dinners made by companies such as Mountain House, Backpacker's Pantry, Natural High, AlpineAire, and more. You can also assemble your own food from the grocery store. You will need to eliminate bulky packaging by condensing food into plastic bags; cut out the cooking instructions and pack in the sealable plastic bags. If you start to backpack on a regular basis, you may enjoy dehydrating your own foods. You can acquire a food dehydrator and vacuum-sealable bags from most hunting supply stores. Experimenting with hiking meals can be fun. Serve your hiker meals for dinner at home. If everyone approves, you have a winning meal! If not, try another entrée. When you hit the trail, always bring along an extra day's worth of food. If you run a day behind schedule or someone eats more than expected, you will have the situation covered, and no one will go hungry.

Backpacking Breakfast Ideas

+ your child's favorite cereal with some powdered milk mixed with water

+ granola bars

+ breakfast fruit bars

+ pancakes (use the batter that just calls for water, and don't forget the syrup)

+ powdered scrambled eggs

+ oatmeal

+ Pop-Tarts

Backpacking Lunch and Snack Ideas

+ bagel peanut butter and jelly sandwiches

+ bagel and honey sandwiches

+ tortilla sandwiches

* cheese and sausage sticks

* foil-wrapped meats (tuna/chicken) and crackers

* energy bars

* candy bars (Snickers is my favorite!)

* dried apples

* dried banana chips

* trail mix (assemble your own favorite mixture)

Backpacking Dinner Ideas

* macaroni and cheese (my kids' favorite!)

* pasta, rice, beans, couscous (anything that can be re-constituted with boiling water)

* freeze-dried meals

* dehydrated fruit and veggies

* foil-wrapped meats (tuna/chicken)

* beef jerky

• • •

Dessert Ideas

* s'mores (marshmallows, chocolate, and graham crackers)

* brownie pies (brownie mix fried in a pan)

* chocolate bars

* cookies

* hot cocoa

Simple sweets (hard candy, foil-wrapped chocolates, and so on) that are small and light make great hiking dessert items.

Protect your food and all scented items (including deodorant, soap, and toothpaste) from bears and other animals. Pack your food in a bear canister or bring a food bag and fifty feet of rope to hang your bear bag at least ten feet in the air and seven feet out from a tree. Some parks require that you keep your food in a bear canister—a container that's the size of a pony keg and is bear-proof. Some parks have installed wire lines between trees or bear poles allowing hikers to hoist their bear bag up without effort, but you should be prepared to hang your own bear bag. If you've never hung a bear bag, you may want to practice this necessary skill at home to get the hang of it. Find two trees fifteen to twenty feet apart. Tie one end of the rope to the base of a tree, and tie the other end of the rope to a weighted object (a rock or a bag with a rock in it, for instance) to throw over a branch that is at least seven feet out from the tree. Repeat this process using a branch on the other tree. Lower the line so you can tie off a loop in the middle, to which you should clip a carabiner. This is what you will clip your bear bag to. You will then hoist the bag high up in the air and tie off the rope to the base of the tree. If you are a visual learner, a quick Internet search of "how to hang a bear bag" will pull up several video links and pictures. Hanging a bear bag is a time-consuming but necessary chore, even for hiking pros.

WHEN I WALKED the Appalachian Trail, I developed an enormous appetite! I could eat a large pizza as a snack before dinner. While visiting with my future wife, Beth, I ate ten and a half donuts before breakfast. Note to self: not a good romantic strategy to impress a future spouse. If I wasn't eating, I was sleeping and dreaming about a juicy steak or walking and salivating about my next meal. A tradition on the Appalachian Trail is to eat a half gallon of ice cream when you reach the halfway point—I enjoyed every bite. Despite my outlandish appetite, I still lost over thirty pounds by the end of my five-million-step journey over two thousand miles. An Appalachian Trail thru-hiker burns four thousand to six thousand calories a day, the equivalency of running two marathons, which explains why I was able to eat so much food while I was on the trail. In addition to my huge appetite, I drank a gallon and a half of water daily. My food and hydration trail habits confirm the importance of keeping our kids hydrated and energized while on the trail.

10

No Bites! No Burn!

Keep Your Kids Safe from Bugs and Sun

When you escape into the great outdoors with your kids, the last thing you want is your child to get eaten alive by bugs or severely sunburned. Not only can hiking fun get derailed by annoying, itching bites from an insect or a painful sunburn, but when a mosquito has the ability to transmit the West Nile virus, a tick can give you Lyme disease or Rocky Mountain spotted fever, and too much sun exposure can result in a deadly form of skin cancer, you need to take precautions. All of this can be alarming, but bugs and sunburn are no reason to call off a hike—especially since a few simple procedures will help keep you and your kids safe.

Modern science has improved our quality of life with products to help keep us safe from all sorts of hazards, including the dangers of bugs and the sun. When I was a child, there were few regulations in place for car seats. Children could ride in the front seat of a car without a seat belt. Try that today and you will be cited and charged with child endangerment. Today, kids ride in the backseat, in government-regulated child seats, surrounded by airbags, and encased with steel door beams, all to protect them in the event of an accident. Much like the child car safety improvements, several innovations have made products available to reduce the risk of acquiring Lyme disease, West Nile virus, and sunburn.

A Multipronged Strategy to Keep the Bugs Away

When I went camping as a kid, Mom would spray us with a coat of DEET bug repellent, and it worked pretty well at keeping the bugs away, though it had an awful chemical odor. Besides the offensive smell, DEET is destructive to synthetic gear and clothing, as I discovered over a five-month period of hiking the Appalachian Trail. As children, our other line of defense to deflect bugs was sitting downwind from the campfire—we were bug-free but inhaling noxious smoke, forcing us to keep our eyes closed. Or in defeat, we would zip into the tent and watch the campfire from the screened window. In recent years, concerns over the safety of high concentrations of DEET have prompted scores of alternative products to hit the marketplace. Yet, despite the worries about DEET and the destructive havoc it can wreak on your gear and clothing, the Centers for Disease Control and Prevention (CDC), the Environmental Protection Agency (EPA), and the American Academy of Pediatrics (AAP) all agree that DEET is safe for use on kids over two months of age. Since the 1950s, DEET has been the most effective repellent, until now.

Picaridin, a relatively new insect repellent, is as effective as DEET in protecting against mosquitos and ticks and has been approved by the EPA and CDC as safe for children two months and older. Like DEET, it is applied to skin and clothing to repel or block insects from biting, but it does not kill insects. Not only do we now have a comparable alternative to DEET, but picaridin is odorless, and it doesn't damage plastics and gear.

An insect repellant containing either picaridin or DEET is your best method to fend off mosquitos, ticks, and other pests that can transmit harmful diseases. Other products such as citronella have not been proven as effective and require many more applications. Always follow the directions on the repellent label. A few general guidelines: when applying repellent, don't apply to your child's hands, eyes or mouth, or on open cuts or scratches. DEET and picaridin are safe on skin but not when swallowed, and younger kids have a tendency to put their hands in their mouths. Apply repellent only to exposed skin. Do not let children apply the repellent themselves. After returning from the hike, be sure to wash the repellent off.

Another product that can protect you from mosquitos and ticks is permethrin. Permethrin is an insecticide that was approved by the EPA for use on clothing, packs, tents, and shoes. It is not for use on skin. Permethrin will stun or kill insects. It is considered safe by the CDC and EPA for use on children's clothing. You can apply it yourself by spraying your clothing with permethrin. Several clothing and gear suppliers are factory-treating items with permethrin.

Since DEET and picaridin are not recommended for children under two months of age, you need to take a few extra precautions with your newborn until the child reaches two months of age. You could simply avoid buggy situations for the first few months, or you could cover your infant carrier with bug netting and check your child for ticks and bites frequently.

Other Methods to Deter Ticks and Mosquito Bites

Wear long-sleeved shirts and pants when tolerable. Stay on the trail and avoid brushing up against plants and logs. Wear light-colored clothing and avoid scented skin lotions and soaps. Avoid hiking at dawn and dusk when bugs are most active. Be sure to check your children for ticks after every hike. Inspect and feel their scalp, underarms, legs, and in and behind ears; do a whole-body and gear check after every hike. Carry a pair of tweezers in your supplies, and brush up on how to safely remove a tick if you find one. Be careful to avoid leaving part of the tick in your skin. Become informed about the symptoms of common bug-borne diseases such as Lyme disease and West Nile virus, so you know what to look for if you or your child experiences an insect bite despite your precautions.

Before we hit the trail we use several methods of bug protection. Since we hike in tick-infested areas, we coat our packs, shoes, tents, and clothing with permethrin (Sawyer or Repel brands). We've found that Natrapel, with the active ingredient picaridin, works great in repelling ticks and mosquitos without the noxious DEET smell. Unlike when using DEET, when using Natrapel we don't have to worry about ruining our clothing or hiking gear. After each hike, we also inspect our kiddos and gear for ticks and wash the repellent off our skin. If we discover a bug bite, we apply some "after bite" skin cream.

+ Important note: The CDC recommends avoiding products that combine bug repellent and sunscreen, mainly because bug repellent usually requires one application whereas sunscreen may require continuous applications.

+ Apply bug repellent first, then sunscreen.

Hiking Fun in the Sun

You need to protect your skin from the sun when hiking. Too much sun exposure can damage your skin and could even result in melanoma, a deadly form of skin cancer. Sun damage comes from exposure to ultraviolet radiation. Even if you are hiking in shaded areas or on a cloudy day, you are still being exposed to the sun's radiation.

Here are a few simple tips that will help keep your family safe from the sun. Check with your pediatrician regarding the use of sunscreen on your child. The AAP recommends avoiding the use of sunscreen on babies less than six months old. The American Academy of Dermatology (AAD) recommends that you should apply at least SPF 30 sunscreen lotion. Look for products that are recommended for kids. Use sunscreen that indicates "broad spectrum," which will protect from both UVA and UVB rays. The waterproof and water-resistant sunscreen will provide better protection as your child sweats or if they plan on swimming. All sunscreen wears off, even the waterproof and water-resistant products, and should be reapplied frequently throughout your time outside—especially after a swim. A good rule of thumb is to reapply sunscreen at least every two hours. Your child's face has sensitive skin. Apply products containing zinc oxide and titanium oxide on their ears, cheeks, and nose. We have been very satisfied with the sunscreen products we use with our kids. We use Coppertone Water Babies and Coppertone Kids, both of which are broad-spectrum, water-resistant, and provide SPF 50 protection. We use Pure & Free Baby Sunblock Stick by Neutrogena on our kids' sensitive facial areas. We also use these same products on our own adult skin; no sense in carrying more than one sunscreen since they work on adults, too!

In addition to sunscreen, or if you have a baby under six months, there are a few more practical solutions to be safe from the sun. Try to stay in the shade as much as possible. Although you can still be exposed to indirect UVB rays in the shade, shady areas do provide some protection from the sun. When comfortable, wear long pants and long-sleeved shirts. You can buy clothing that protects you from the sun. Look for the ultraviolet protection factor (UPF) on the label. UPF ratings are similar to SPF ratings of sunscreen. Condition your child to wear a wide-brimmed hat, to cover the ears and neck. Some kids, including my own, will prefer a baseball hat, so be sure to apply sunscreen to the exposed ears and neck. Your child's eyes are prone to sun damage, too, so shop for sunglasses that protect from UVA and UVB rays.

These practical steps will keep your whole family bug- and burn-free while trekking. I'm sure you can recall a time or two where you were eaten alive by mosquitos or were red as a lobster from sunburn. Nothing can ruin outdoor fun quite so quickly. Today, we have so many scientifically proven products and strategies at our fingertips, and we should use them to keep our kids safe as they learn to navigate the great outdoors.

WHEN YOU THINK of the dangers of hiking, ticks usually aren't the first thing you think of. But you should. These little buggers can get into the most discrete places on your body, and if you don't have someone along to spot and remove them, they'll embed themselves—and you stand the risk of contracting Lyme disease. While I was hiking the Appalachian Trail, I didn't have a partner to check me over for ticks. I had to do this myself, which can be a challenge. On one of my town stops along the trail, I took lodging at a hotel. When I checked into my room, I called my parents and left the hotel phone number on their voice mail. While I was in the shower, I heard the phone ringing. I dashed out of the shower and answered the phone. As I stood there dripping wet in my birthday suit talking to my mom, I looked up at the mirror in front of me, which was showing a reflection of another mirror behind me. I noticed an unusual dark dot on my behind that I had never seen before. After hanging up the phone, I removed a tick from my backside and I placed it in a sealable bag to preserve for Lyme disease testing if necessary. I removed the tick in time and thankfully never contracted Lyme disease. If I hadn't checked into that hotel and noticed the tick, it could have infected me.

Other resources:

Centers for Disease Control and Prevention: "Spring and Summer Outdoor Safety," www.cdc.gov/Features/ MovingOutdoors

National Pesticide Information Center: "Picaridin General Fact Sheet," http://npic.orst.edu/factsheets/ PicaridinGen.html

Skin Cancer Foundation: "Sun Protection," www.skincancer .org/prevention/sun-protection

11

Becoming a Seasoned Hiking Caregiver

Some Skills and a Little Knowledge Can Go a Long Way on the Trail

You don't need to be a seasoned outdoor pro to hit the trail with your kids, but having some safety skills, safety gear, and outdoor knowledge tucked away could make the difference between a fun hike and a hiking disaster. Whenever you begin anything new, there are always skills and knowledge to learn. That's part of the adventure. However, when you head down the trail, basic conveniences such as dialing 911 or stopping to ask for directions if you're lost are no longer options. It's up to you to respond to an emergency and navigate on your own. Keeping everyone safe, healthy, and informed is your responsibility. Additionally, when you step into the forest, you are entering the home of countless wild creatures and exposing yourself to nature's elements. The great outdoors is a fragile home to many species and requires your help in protecting it. Modeling appropriate etiquette in the outdoors will teach your kids to do the same. Inherently, encounters with some of these wild creatures can pose a risk, as can weather and terrain. If you plan to hike with your kids in remote wilderness areas, a few key steps will prepare you for your adventure.

Always Leave Your Itinerary and Contact Information with Someone You Trust

Before you head out on your adventure, always alert someone you know and trust (parents, siblings, friends) of your travel plans, even if your adventure is to a nearby destination. If you get lost or injured, this simple step will set a search and rescue in motion in a timely manner. Hikers, including seasoned pros, get lost and injured in the woods all the time, even just short distances from domestic amenities. Informing someone you trust and making that a simple routine, by using a communication mode you're comfortable with—e-mail, text, handwritten note, or voice mail—could be a lifesaving step. Be sure to include pertinent information such as what trail you plan to hike, where you plan to leave your vehicle, when you plan to return, when your trusted person should contact authorities if you haven't returned, and emergency park contact information. If something doesn't go as planned, this will expedite getting search and rescue professionals to your location.

Take an Orienteering Course: Learn How to Use a Compass, a Map, and a GPS

Do you know how to use a map and compass? GPS systems are becoming more prevalent in the backcountry, but what if the device's battery dies or the GPS breaks from a fall or it's submerged in a lake? Navigating with a compass and map isn't difficult; it just takes a little practice. This can be a fun pre-trip endeavor. Look for orienteering course offerings in your area—many county or metro parks offer such courses for free or a nominal fee. Look up orienteering clubs in your area to view their schedule of competitions. Most of these groups welcome novices and new members to their events. Additionally, letterboxing is a fun treasure-hunting game that uses compass skills to find hidden caches in public parks and areas. For more information and to find letterboxes in your area, go to www.letterboxing.org. You should practice using your GPS device as well. Like letterboxing, geocaching is a popular GPS treasure-finding game that will help you get comfortable with your GPS. You can read all about it on the official website: www.geocaching.com. When you are hiking, two simple strategies will keep you from getting lost: First, stay on the trail. Second, every time you reach a trail junction, double-check your map to make sure you choose the right path.

Know How to Signal for Help If You Get Lost or Injured

If you get lost and off course, backtrack or stay put. Don't continue drifting deeper into the forest if you are off the trail. Carry a whistle and a signal mirror, and provide your kids with them as well. Teach your children to blow their whistle if they get into trouble. The sound of a whistle blast will carry much farther than yelling and is more likely to be heard from a long distance. Pilots are trained to look for signal reflections along with other emergency signals. The universal distress signal is any pattern of *three*: three whistle blasts, three mirror reflection signals, three columns of smoke emitting from fires in a clearing, three piles of rocks, or three bright pieces of clothing in a clearing. If you get into an emergency situation, be creative—it could save your life.

Brush up on how to make an emergency shelter and a fire. If you are injured or lost, staying comfortable and dry is important. Some of your gear, such as an emergency rain poncho and your hiking poles, can be modified into a shelter or lean-to. Even if you are not planning on backpacking overnight, carry some waterproof matches and a lighter to help build a fire.

A new device growing in popularity among outdoor adventurers is the SPOT Personal Tracker. This device uses satellite communication to initiate a rescue with a push of a button. You can read more about this device on SPOT's website, www.findmespot.com.

Take Practical Steps to Avoid Danger and Injury

Animal Encounters

The likelihood of a dangerous animal encounter is rare, but it can happen. When you are planning your adventure, research the types of animals you might encounter in the area where you plan to hike. Follow safety regulations and recommendations from local officials and experts, and don't take foolish risks.

Black bears widely populate the United States and other countries, making the opportunity to see one in the wild very likely. This can be an amazing experience for your family if you take a few precautions. Black bears vary in appearance and aggressiveness, depending on where you're hiking. Therefore, parks have varying rules regarding food storage and etiquette tailored to their specific bear population. The local park rangers and authorities will have the best information on the bears based on current happenings. Heed their advice. The following paragraphs provide some general precautions.

Always secure your food and scented items (toothpaste, lotions, deodorants, soaps) using the locally recommended bear-safe method. This may involve using a bear canister, hanging the items in a bag ten feet in the air between two trees, hanging your bear bag on a park-installed mechanism, or storing your items in a bear-proof storage locker.

If a black bear comes into your camp, it is probably looking for food. Gather up your kids, back away slowly, and, most important, don't try to save the food. Keep everyone together, bang metal objects together, and make yourself look as big as possible by waving your arms. Talk firmly and calmly to the bear so that it knows you're human; they have poor vision. If a bear stands up on two legs, don't be alarmed, it's just trying to get a better sense of you. Face the bear, but never stare it down; it may perceive this as a challenge. If the bear continues to pursue you instead of the food, use bear spray if you have it and fight back by throwing rocks, sticks, your pack, or whatever you have, but don't run or turn away. Bears can run thirty miles an hour, and they will think you are prey if you turn and run. Black bears are excellent tree climbers, so forget about climbing a tree as a way of escape. Continue to stand your ground and fight back if the bear attacks. Black bears have been known to discontinue attacking humans when they fight back. The chance of a bear attack is extremely rare, but having a rehearsed plan may decrease your anxiety and will increase your ability to prevent an injury.

Before hitting the trail, talk to your kids about what to do if you encounter a bear in the wild. Hike in a group of four or more. Stay together in bear country. Sing songs, talk continuously, or tie bells to your boots to alert the bears of your presence. This will reduce the chances of surprising a bear, which could cause a defensive attack. Bears are solitary animals and would prefer not to encounter people, so these measures could prevent an encounter before it happens. If you do encounter a bear, instruct your kids to never run but instead to back away slowly toward their parents and wait for parental instructions. Keep your kids together with you. Pick up your little ones. If you see a bear from a safe distance and the bear pays no attention to you, enjoy this rare experience from a safe distance. Do not encroach on the bears for a photo; use your zoom lens instead. Never offer food to a bear. Be mindful that a mother bear will do everything to protect her cubs, so if you find yourself close to a bear cub, back away so that you are not between momma and her babies.

Grizzly bears will react differently to a human encounter than will their black bear cousins. If you plan to hike in grizzly bear country, carry bear pepper spray and familiarize yourself with how to use it. All of the precautions mentioned for a black bear encounter apply for a grizzly encounter except in the instance of the bear attacking or charging. If a grizzly bear is pursuing you or an attack is imminent, spray pepper spray if you have it. Do not fight back; unlike a black bear, a grizzly will not be deterred and you will lose. If the bear continues to pursue you, grab your child and drop to the ground in the prone position and play dead, with your child beneath you. The bear will think you are dead or nonthreatening, even if you were just standing moments before. Keep your pack on to protect your back from its claws, and cover your neck with your hands. Do not move or make a sound—take the pain. A grizzly will leave you alone after nudging you around and assuming you are dead. Remain in that position and don't make one peep or move until you are absolutely sure the bear has left the area.

Mountain lions thrive in many of the western US states and can pose a risk to hikers. If you are in mountain lion country, hike in groups and never let your children roam free. A mountain lion encounter is extremely rare, so if you encounter one, assume that it's stalking you. Pick up your kids while facing the lion and have your older children stand behind you. Wave your hands above your head to look as big as possible. Never bend down. Talk loudly and firmly so it knows you're human. Throw rocks and sticks at the lion, and never turn your back or run. Spray pepper spray if you have it. Fight back with everything you've got if it attacks.

Mountain lions and grizzly bears live in pockets of the United States. Mountain lions are more prevalent than grizzly bears, whereas black bears reside in almost every region of the country. Prior to your adventure, check the park website, park literature, and with the park rangers on what animals exist there and what precautions to take.

Weather, Terrain, and High-Water Precautions

Lean on the side of safety when previewing the weather, terrain, and waterways. Check the weather forecast before you hit the trail. If there is a strong chance of thunderstorms and your route takes you across an open plain or above the trees, wait out the storm or take a different route. You are more prone to lightning strikes when you are the tallest object in the area or if you are near metal objects (like hiking poles). If an unseasonable snowstorm is looming, call off the hike. Avoid trails that require fording streams until your children are older and capable of crossing them. Excessive rain or torrential downpours can cause high water and flash floods. A bubbling brook can become a dangerous river in a short time. A dried-up riverbed can become an instant wall of water crashing down the mountain, swooping up anything in its path. Err on the side of safety. If the local authorities recommend postponing your adventure, heed their advice.

Snakes, Poison Ivy, and Other Off-Trail Dangers

One simple piece of advice will prevent potentially unpleasant encounters: *Stay on the trail!* A well-maintained trail is clear of rocks, logs, poison ivy, underbrush, and tall grass where snakes can be found. Snakes are more afraid of you than you are of them, but when you leave the trail, you may potentially brush past a rock with a snake behind it or scrape against poison ivy. Stopping to use the bathroom or to get water and other such scenarios will require that you step off the trail. When you do, be mindful of where you're stepping. Never blindly reach under or behind rocks and logs where a snake or other creature might be.

Prepare Yourself for Unexpected Emergencies

When you head off down the trail, you are exposing yourself and your children to everything Mother Nature has to
offer. Hitting the trail with your kids is a healthy endeavor,
but you need to be prepared for the medical emergencies
and medical conditions that can occur from the environment and conditions in which you are hiking. If your child
has any medical issues, check with your pediatrician before
heading out on your adventure. Bring along your children's
medicine and any prescriptions they might be taking. Acclimate yourself with the closest medical facilities available to
the area where you will be.

First Aid

Outfit a first-aid kit for all potential issues. We pack a first-
aid kit for a family of four made by Adventure Medical
Kits. In addition to all the standard items in the first-aid
kit, such as bandages, first-aid tape, pain reliever, tweezers,
and ice packs, we add items customized to our own family's
needs. Be sure to pack along first-aid items to address high-
frequency hiking issues with kids. Moleskin is a must-have
to treat blisters. Be sure to pack antibiotic ointment and
supplies to clean cuts and wounds. Pack plenty of Band-Aids
to help sooth your children's hurts and owies. Pack along
some anti-itch cream (hydrocortisone) for poison ivy and
rashes, as well as some Afterbite cream for that bug bite.
Pack along tweezers to remove slivers and ticks. Take a Red
Cross class to brush up on first-aid procedures.

Children, especially infants, are more prone to weather-
and temperature-related illnesses than adults are. Brush up

on the signs, symptoms, prevention, and treatment of hypothermia, heat exhaustion, sunstroke, and dehydration. These conditions can be prevented and have recognizable symptoms. A dramatic shift in your child's behavior is a red flag that something is wrong.

Hypothermia

When your body temperature drops below 95 degrees Fahrenheit, hypothermia occurs. Hypothermia can set in even in moderate temperatures. Cold and wet conditions can cause hypothermia, but the temperature doesn't have to be below freezing. Kids may not complain of anything being wrong. Some early signs are shivering and confusion. You can prevent hypothermia by dressing your child in non cotton layers and by keeping them dry. In cool temperatures, make sure they wear hats and gloves, even if they complain. Kids lose heat faster than adults do, so add extra layers. Take frequent snack breaks and drink plenty of water. If your child exhibits some of the early symptoms, get him out of the elements, replace his wet clothes with dry ones, and encourage him to drink a hot drink such as hot chocolate. Warm him up with your own body heat by zipping up together in a sleeping bag. Hypothermia, if left untreated, can rapidly worsen and is fatal. Seek medical attention if necessary.

Dehydration, Heat Exhaustion, and Sunstroke

Kids, as well as adults, are at risk of losing water and electrolytes while hiking. Some early indicators of this are fatigue; lack of urination; or dark-colored, smelly urine. You can prevent dehydration by encouraging your child to drink often. Take frequent breaks. Stop and sip water every ten or fifteen minutes. A hydration hose system makes it easy for your child to drink and encourages frequent sips as you hike along. Mix Pedialyte or Gatorade with your child's water.

Avoid hiking in the middle of the day, when the temperatures are the hottest. Get out of the sun with every opportunity. Dehydration can lead to heat exhaustion or sunstroke. If your child exhibits dizziness or cramps along with fatigue, he most likely has heat exhaustion. Get him into the shade, out of the sun, and encourage him to sip water, Gatorade, or Pedialyte. Postpone the hike until he feels better and is fully hydrated. Heat exhaustion can lead to heatstroke, a dangerous condition where the body temperature rises above normal. Symptoms of heatstroke are confusion, irrational behavior, unconsciousness, elevated pulse, increased body temperature, and hot skin. Get him to a shaded area, loosen all clothing, and put cold packs under his arms and at his groin area. Discontinue the cold packs if he begins to shiver. Encourage water intake if he is alert. Elevate his feet with a rolled-up coat or pack to keep blood flowing to the brain. Alert park authorities or medical personnel of your emergency.

This information is just an overview of some of the more common issues that can occur to hikers in remote wilderness areas. Reading this brief explanation of hypothermia, dehydration, heat exhaustion, and sunstroke does not qualify or certify anyone to provide care for someone exhibiting these conditions. This information is provided to increase your awareness of some of the dangerous medical conditions to be aware of before you head into the great outdoors with your kids so you can seek further training and advice to respond appropriately if an emergency does occur.

Get Your Wilderness First-Aid and CPR Certification

Do you have the skills to respond to a medical emergency? As a parent or caregiver, a general first-aid and CPR course would be beneficial for unexpected emergencies. Most communities offer several courses specific to the outdoors, such as, Wilderness First Aid, First Aid: When Help Is Delayed, and Wilderness First Responder. Check with your local Red Cross for more information on available classes. One emergency will make you very grateful you took the time to gain some skills and knowledge in how to respond.

Teach Your Kids to Leave the Environment as They Found It

Wilderness is fragile. Whenever you head into the back-country with your children, you are modeling behaviors that your kids will learn from and imitate. Technological advances offer us lots of innovative ways to protect the environment. Antibacterial sanitizer gel provides a way for a hiker to clean her hands after using the bathroom or before meals in the woods, without polluting the stream with soap. Teaching your child to use a digital camera is a fun way for her to take nothing from the woods but pictures and memories. Your children's witnessing you pick up a piece of trash on the trail and put it in your own trash bag or your going the proper distance from the trail and the water to use the bathroom will leave a lasting impression on how to treat the environment.

The National Park Service, Boy Scouts of America, and many other outdoor organizations encourage the seven

Leave No Trace principles. Every hiker and anyone spending time in the great outdoors should learn these guidelines.

THE LEAVE NO TRACE SEVEN PRINCIPLES*

✤ Plan Ahead and Prepare.

✤ Travel and Camp on Durable Surfaces.

✤ Dispose of Waste Properly.

✤ Leave What You Find.

✤ Minimize Campfire Impacts.

✤ Respect Wildlife.

✤ Be Considerate of Other Visitors.

*The member-driven Leave No Trace Center for Outdoor Ethics teaches people how to enjoy the outdoors responsibly. This copyrighted information has been reprinted with permission from the Leave No Trace Center for Outdoor Ethics.

The Ten Essentials—Learn How to Use Them!*

If you ask a sampling of seasoned hikers to empty out their packs and show you what they take with them on every hike, you are sure to get a wide variety of items. Even so, you will always find several items in every seasoned hiker's pack known as the Ten Essentials.

The point of the Ten Essentials list (developed by the Mountaineers, with origins in the climbing course taught by the Club since the 1930s) has always been to help answer two basic questions: First, can you respond positively to an accident or emergency? Second, can you safely spend a night—or more—out? The list has evolved over time from a list of individual items to a list of functional systems.

TEN ESSENTIALS: THE CLASSIC LIST*

1. Map
2. Compass
3. Sunglasses and sunscreen
4. Extra clothing
5. Headlamp/flashlight
6. First-aid supplies
7. Fire starter
8. Matches
9. Knife
10. Extra food

*The "Ten Essentials" was reprinted with permission from *Mountaineering: The Freedom of the Hills.*

TEN ESSENTIAL SYSTEMS

1. Navigation (map and compass)
2. Sun protection (sunglasses and sunscreen)
3. Insulation (extra clothing)
4. Illumination (headlamp/flashlight)
5. First-aid supplies
6. Fire (waterproof matches/lighter/candle)
7. Repair kit and tools

8. Nutrition (extra food)
9. Hydration (extra water)
10. Emergency shelter (tent/plastic tube tent/garbage bag)

1. Navigation

Always carry a detailed topographic map of the area you are visiting, and place it in a protective case or plastic covering. Always carry a compass. Climbers may also choose to carry other navigational tools such as an altimeter or GPS receiver; other aids include route markers, route descriptions, and other types of maps or photos.

2. Sun Protection

Carry and use sunglasses, sunscreen for the lips and skin, and clothing for sun protection.

3. Insulation (Extra Clothing)

How much extra clothing is necessary for an emergency? The garments used during the active portion of a climb and considered to be the basic climbing outfit include inner and outer socks, boots, underwear, pants, shirt, sweater or fleece jacket, hat, mittens or gloves, and raingear. The term "extra clothing" refers to additional layers that would be needed to survive the long, inactive hours of an unplanned bivouac.

4. Illumination

Even if the climbing party plans to return to their cars before dark, it is essential to carry a headlamp or flashlight, just in case. Batteries and bulbs do not last forever, so carry spares of both at all times.

5. First-Aid Supplies

Carry and know how to use a first-aid kit, but do not let a first-aid kit give you a false sense of security. The best course of action is to always take the steps necessary to avoid injury or sickness in the first place. At a minimum, a first-aid kit should include gauze pads in various sizes, roller gauze, small adhesive bandages, butterfly bandages, triangular bandages, battle dressing (or Carlisle bandage), adhesive tape, scissors, cleansers or soap, latex gloves, and paper and pencil.

6. Fire

Carry the means to start and sustain an emergency fire. Most climbers carry a butane lighter or two, instead of matches, in a waterproof container. Either must be absolutely reliable. Fire starters are indispensable for igniting wet wood quickly to make an emergency campfire. Common fire starters include candles, chemical heat tabs, and canned heat. On a high-altitude snow or glacier climb where firewood is nonexistent, it is advisable to carry a stove as an additional emergency heat and water source.

7. Repair Kit and Tools

Knives are so useful in first aid, food preparation, repairs, and climbing that every party member needs to carry one. Leashes to prevent loss are common. Other tools (pliers, screwdriver, awl, scissors) can be part of a knife or a pocket tool, or carried separately—perhaps even as part of a group kit. Other useful repair items are shoelaces, safety pins, needle and thread, wire, duct tape, nylon fabric repair tape, cable ties, plastic buckles, cordage, webbing, and parts for equipment such as tent, stove, crampons, snowshoes, and skis.

8. Nutrition (Extra Food)

For shorter trips, a one-day supply of extra food is a reasonable emergency stockpile in case foul weather, faulty navigation, injury, or other reasons delay the planned return. An expedition or long trek may require more. The food should require no cooking, be easily digestible, and store well for long periods. A combination of jerky, nuts, candy, granola, and dried fruit works well. If a stove is carried, cocoa, dried soup, and tea can be added. There are many possibilities.

9. Hydration (Extra Water)

Carry extra water and have the skills and tools required for obtaining and purifying additional water. Always carry at least one water bottle or collapsible water sack. Daily water consumption varies greatly. Two quarts (liters) daily is a reasonable minimum; in hot weather or at high altitudes, 6 quarts may not be enough. In dry environments, carry additional water. Plan for enough water to accommodate additional requirements due to heat, cold, altitude, exertion, or emergency.

10. Emergency Shelter

If the climbing party is not carrying a tent, carry some sort of extra shelter from rain and wind, such as a plastic tube tent or a jumbo plastic trash bag. Another possibility is a reflective emergency blanket. It can be used in administering first aid to an injured or hypothermic person and can double as a means of shelter.

"The Ten Essentials" Classic list and The Ten Essential System lists are reprinted from *Mountaineering: The Freedom of the Hills*, 8th edition, with permission from the publisher, The Mountaineers, Seattle, Washington.

WEATHER CONDITIONS CAN change dramatically on the trail. You should always be prepared with the right clothing and brush up your knowledge of symptoms of illness related to weather exposure and what to do in such a scenario. Several years ago, a friend and I took a day hike up to the Mount LeConte shelter, the highest shelter in the Great Smoky Mountains National Park at 6,440 feet in elevation. It was early April. When we left Gatlinburg, the sun was shining and people were wearing shorts. We drove up the mountain to the Alum Cave Trailhead parking lot. When we started hiking, the sun had been replaced by clouds, the temperature was much cooler than it was in Gatlinburg, and it started to rain. As we continued our hike, the rain turned to sleet and then to snow. We were dressed in synthetic layers and stopped to put on our waterproof, breathable rain parkas. We were just out on a day hike and planned to return to Gatlinburg after stopping at the shelter for lunch. When we entered the shelter, we encountered a family of four standing beneath the shelter roof with their backpacks lying on the ground. They had arrived at the shelter moments before we showed up. The parents and the two children were shivering and just standing, staring out at the falling snow. They appeared to be suffering from the early symptoms of hypothermia. All four family members were wearing throwaway plastic rain parkas on top of cotton T-shirts and jeans. Their clothes were soaking wet. The father, as he stood beside his shivering wife and children, explained between chattering teeth that this was his family's first overnight hike. My friend and I asked them if they had any extra dry clothes they could put on. The father nodded and began fumbling with his backpack straps, popping open the top pouch and pulling out some clothes. We instructed the family to remove their wet clothes and put on dry ones, turning away to give them some privacy. After the family had changed out of their cold, wet cotton clothes, life seemed to come back to all of them. They began to talk to us more fluidly. We asked them if they had a backpacking stove and the father pulled one out of his pack. We helped assemble the stove and boiled some water and served the family some hot cocoa. I gave them a few of my trail energy bars to snack on and they gobbled those down. We suggested that they all zip into their sleeping bags to stay warm, which they immediately did.

Some other hikers arrived to stay the night at the shelter. These hikers were seasoned, and we had a discussion about the hypothermic symptoms the family of four displayed when we first encountered them. The family was acting normal now; they all insisted they were warm and comfortable as they lay in their sleeping bags. With dusk approaching and snow falling, everyone agreed that staying the night in the shelter and heading down the mountain to their car in the morning was their best option—especially with two young children who had already exerted themselves with a five-mile hike up the mountain. The seasoned group of hikers said they would hike out with the family in the morning and make sure everyone was okay. My friend and I didn't have overnight supplies, so after we were assured that this family was going to be okay, we hiked back to our car. If this family hadn't encountered anyone else on that hike, the scenario could've played out much differently.

Other resources:

The National Park Service website: www.nps.gov/index.htm

The Leave No Trace seven principles: www.lnt.org

Bear spray information: www.epa.gov/region8/toxics/pests/
beardeter.html

12

Everything but the Kitchen Sink!

Clothing, Packs, Footwear, Sleeping Bags,
Stoves, and More

Now that you've made plans to take your kids hiking or backpacking, you need to assemble the necessary clothing and gear. Hiking can be one of the least expensive hobbies and sports. All you really need is a good pair of shoes, some basic survival essentials, and a pack. It can get expensive if you want all the latest gear and gadgets. Even so, children will outgrow their clothing, packs, and footwear, requiring you to continually upgrade to fit their size, but the rest of the equipment can last a lifetime. The appendixes of this book contain gear checklists to help you organize for your hike. In this chapter, I've assembled some essential information to consider as you purchase and acquire your clothing and gear.

Dress Your Child with the Right Clothing for Your Hike!

Assembling the appropriate clothing for your child is very important. The wrong type of clothing can become a major issue in various climates and weather conditions. As mentioned in previous chapters, the first rule of thumb is—NO COTTON! Cotton retains moisture, which can lower your body temperature, and it can cause a rash or chafing. Dress your child in layers of non cotton wicking, breathable clothing. There are three essential layers of clothing: the base layer, middle layer (insulating), and the outer layer. The base layer is the clothing directly up against your skin: underwear, long underwear, shirt, and socks. Fabrics such as silk, wool, or synthetics like polypropylene (polypro), Capilene, or polyester make a good base layer that will wick perspiration away from your skin to the outer layers, where it will evaporate. The middle/insulating layer will vary depending on climate and season. Think of the middle layer as your hiking outfit. Fabrics that work well for this layer are nylon, wool, fleece, polyester, Capilene, and other lightweight, non cotton wicking items. This could be as simple as your shorts or pants and shirt for a warm-weather hike, or it could be an insulating layer of fleece, wool, or a pile jacket and pants during cold weather. Fleece is available in varying degrees of thickness. You can add or remove this layer as you heat up or cool down. Think of the outer layer as the shell protecting the turtle. This is the layer that protects you from rain, wind, and snow. Select a waterproof, breathable rain parka and pants. Look for GORE-TEX or comparable (waterproof/breathable) labels. Pack according to season. The idea of layering applies to your outer extremities (hands, feet, and head) as well. Be sure to pack along wool or synthetic gloves and a hat, and in extreme cold conditions, you may want additional layers of socks.

When packing for your child, be sure to bring along a few pairs of extra socks and one or two extra outfits. If your child gets cold or wet, you want to be able to change her out of her wet items into something dry. If you are backpacking, you can use the second outfit for your child's nighttime clothing.

A bandana is a very useful item to bring on a hike. It is the only cotton item I bring on a hike. A bandana can filter debris out of water, and it can be used as a washcloth, a head cover, a first-aid tourniquet, a tissue, and more. The usefulness of a bandana is limited only by your imagination.

Here are a few more tips to consider as you acquire your children's hiking clothes. Nylon hiking pants are available with an option to zip off the legs and convert them to shorts. This feature allows the pants to serve a dual purpose and allows you to pack light. You can also buy clothing that protects your child from the sun. Look for the Ultra violet Protection Factor (UPF), which is similar to SPF ratings of sunscreen, on the label. Some outdoor clothing items manufactured by ExOfficio and Columbia have been factory-treated with bug repellent that lasts up to seventy washes. As of this printing, the bug-repelling outdoor clothing is available only in adult sizes. Stay tuned for wicking, bug-repellent-treated outdoor clothing for kids.

CLOTHING LIST

❧ rain jacket

❧ underwear

* socks

* pants

* shorts

* shirt

* gloves

* hat

* bandanna

Money-saving tip: Try to purchase neutral colors of clothing that can be handed down to either gender (you may not want to dress your son in a pink, flowered shirt!). We chose a yellow rain parka and pants for our daughter, and we were able to pass them on to our son. Check secondhand stores for synthetic clothing. If you know someone who is handy with a sewing machine, you could have them make you a few baby outfits out of some of your old hiking garments.

Footwear

The most important asset for hikers is their feet. Your child's footwear needs will evolve as she grows. The first few years, birth to three, you will be the primary walker, and you can accomodate your child's footwear needs with a pair of comfortable, water-resistant baby/toddler shoes. As your child begins hiking consistently on his own two feet, around age three, you want to make sure he has some good walking shoes. A pair of well-fitted running or gym shoes will do the trick. Hiking-specific footwear may be hard to find for the younger ages. If you do find hiking shoes, look for a sturdy sole (I recommend Vibram, if available) and waterproof, breathable fabric (such as GORE-TEX). If you can't find waterproof, breathable footwear, just be sure the shoe or liner fabric is not cotton, and use non cotton, wicking socks.

As your child increases his walking miles, good footwear becomes more essential than ever, and luckily, the older he gets, the more readily available hiking footwear will become. Get your kids properly fitted by an outfitter that specializes in hiking. A good outfitter will fit your child into footwear with consideration given to the terrain you plan to hike, the extra weight you plan to carry in your pack, and, of course, a comfortable fit. Most of your kids' hiking footwear needs will be satisfied with hiking shoes or midcut boots.

Hiking footwear, or I should say *hiking footwear philosophy*, has lightened up significantly over the years. Gone is the mentality that you need to wrap your feet in thick, heavy leather boots. Now, the majority of hikers are wearing trail shoes and midcut over-the-ankle boots made of lightweight synthetic material that is both wicking and waterproof. Heavy leather boots and mountaineering boots still have their place for more extreme use, but for general trail hiking, lighter-weight shoes or boots are best. Trail shoes and lightweight boots are more comfortable and require minimal break-in. You are, however, more prone to rolling your ankle, and the lower cut means more trail debris in your boot.

Finding a brand that fits well on your child is an individual pursuit. One brand may work great on one kid, but not on another. You should acquire your footgear well in advance of your hike and wear it around, simulating the terrain in which you will hike. If your footwear causes you any problems, take it back. You don't want to get to your destination and have to deal with painful blisters. The two main issues that cause blisters are friction and moisture. So you want a secure-fitting, comfortable shoe or boot paired with wicking socks.

Your footwear isn't complete without a few accessories. In addition to your child's hiking shoes, invest in a pair of sandals or Crocs to wear around camp to let your little hiker's feet breathe. As mentioned in a previous chapter, be sure to outfit your first-aid kit with moleskin, to treat any blisters that occur. Bring along two or three pairs of socks to help keep your little one's feet warm and dry. Invest in a pair of gaiters to further protect your child's feet and shins. Gaiters are a synthetic fabric wrapping that covers your socks and the tops of your trail shoes, keeping out debris and moisture. They are available in a low or high cut. The high-cut gaiters will protect your legs from cuts and scrapes. Gaiters also give you an added layer of protection against ticks.

Packs

Your pack needs will change several times as your child grows. Some of this information was stated in the chapters for each age range. All of the pack tips are compiled below by age range.

Infant Carrier—Birth to Six Months

From birth to six months, you will need a front-loading infant carrier or a sling. Two brands to consider that lead the industry are Ergobaby and Baby Björn. These are available from most stores that sell baby products and from some backpacking outfitters.

Child Carrier—Six Months to Three Years

When your child has adequate neck support, usually around six months, they will be ready for a backpack child carrier. The marketplace is riddled with such child carriers, but backpack manufacturers make some of the best available. Some brands to look for are Kelty, Deuter, and Osprey. You want to be sure to select a pack that is comfortable for your child and for you. A good outfitter can help you fit into the right pack. Many of the same considerations used to fit you into a traditional backpack apply to a child carrier. Some of these considerations include the following:

* torso length

* waist size

* gender

* cubic inches of storage space

Child carriers have a harness system similar to a car seat that allows for growth. Some additional features to look for include the following:

* Does the pack have a sun/rain/weather cover?

* Is the gear storage area adequate for all your supplies?

* Does my child fit safely into the carrier?

Adventure Pack—Ages Three to Five

By the time your child is three, she is most likely hiking short distances, and you will want to fit her with a small adventure pack. This can be a simple backpack so your little gal can carry along a toy, a magnifying glass, a bug catcher, or other fun items to interact with the great outdoors.

Day Pack—Five Years to Teenage

By the age of five, the adventure fun pack has run its course. If your kid can carry a school book bag, he is ready for a backpack that can hold real provisions. You can get away with a school book bag with the five- to seven-year-olds for lightweight loads, but you will want to acquire a more durable hiking brand of day pack with a hip belt, sternum strap, and hydration hose capability for the older child. Visit an outfitter to properly fit your child into a good day pack.

Trekking Poles

Kids can benefit from trekking poles. Trekking poles, which look similar to ski poles, provide added balance and stability. They move the hiking workout to the upper body, taking the impact off your ankles and knees. They can help keep you balanced while fording streams, serve as a shelter pole, and store duct tape by wrapping it around the shaft, just below the handles. You will need to spend some time teaching your children how to use the poles safely. Adjustable poles will last through adulthood. You will need to set the pole height so that your child can comfortably grip the handles while extending his arm out at a 90-degree angle. Visit an outfitter for this purchase. Trekking poles have several features, such as shock absorption capability, various lock mechanisms, and grips, to name a few. Your kid may not need all the bells and whistles, but she will need a quality pole from a reputable manufacturer.

Accessories

Compass and GPS

A compass will help you navigate your way when paired with a topographical map. GPS devices are becoming more commonplace. Be sure to bring along some backup batteries. You should learn how to use your compass by participating in an orienteering group.

Knife

A multipurpose knife, such as the classic Swiss Army knife, can perform a variety of functions on a hike, from cutting moleskin, repairing a broken piece of gear, or simply slicing a piece of cheese for lunch. If your model has tweezers, you can use them to remove a tick or a splinter. You should also carry a small locking-blade survival knife for instances of chopping, prying, or digging. Knives should be carried by the adults and older children, parent permitting, who have demonstrated the ability to use the knife properly.

Matches and Lighter

Pack along two fire-starter sources. You never know when you might need to make a fire to keep warm or to cook dinner. A few boxes of waterproof matches and a lighter will do the trick. Keep them in a sealable plastic bag. The adults or an older child, parent permitting, should carry the matches and lighters.

Whistle

Always carry a whistle in case you have an emergency and need to sound an alert for help. A whistle burst can travel farther than your voice. Three whistle blasts is the universal distress signal.

First-Aid Kit

Pack along a first-aid kit with enough supplies for the entire hiking party. I carry a first-aid kit for a family of four, made by Adventure Medical Kits, but you can assemble your own. Be sure to include Band-Aids, first-aid antibiotic ointment, moleskin, tweezers, pain-reliever medicine, Benadryl, and so forth.

Duct Tape

Duct tape is one of the most useful items in my backpack.

You can repair torn clothes and boots, repair a pack, patch a leaky hydration hose, or doctor a blister with duct tape. Entire books have been written about the many creative uses of duct tape. Wrap a piece of duct tape four to six inches long around a small piece of cardboard, the shaft of your hiking pole, or around your water bottle. You never know when you might need it.

Additional Items for Overnight Backpacking

If you plan on backpacking overnight, you will need some gear in addition to the items that have already been mentioned.

Backpack—Seven Years to Teenage

By the age of seven or eight a child can carry some of their own backpacking supplies. As a rule of thumb, a child should not carry more than twenty percent of his body weight. Just as you do for your own excursions, you will need to fit your child properly into a pack. There are many factors that go into a backpack decision, and an outfitter that specializes in backpacking supplies can best meet your child's needs. A pack-fitting specialist will measure your child's torso and hip size. She will inquire about your pack needs: size of pack (cubic inches or liters) and internal or external frame. Internal frames conform to your body and are good for rugged trails requiring free range of movement. External frame packs are designed for heavier loads, but they don't have the free movement agility of the internal frame. Try to find a pack that offers room to grow. Most packs adjust easily. The pack specialist will load the pack with the approximate weight that your child will carry on your excursion. Make sure the pack fits correctly and is comfortable on your child. After all the straps (hip belt, shoulder straps, load-lifter straps, sternum straps, and stabilizer straps) are tightened, does the weight of the pack rest primarily on her hips? Is the shoulder strap snug over her shoulders? Can she walk with the pack? Ask your child how it feels. It may take some time to find the right pack, but it's worth it if you plan to do some overnight backpacking. Be sure to add in a backpack rain cover. Believe it or not, packs are not waterproof.

Sleeping Bags

Choose the right sleeping bag for your journey. Finding a good, compact, child-size sleeping bag might be difficult. You may be better off purchasing an adult-size bag and letting your child grow into it. Sleeping bags are made of all sorts of fabrics and fibers. They vary in size and shape and are designed for different climates and functions. Most backpacking sleeping bags are the mummy design, which allows you to wrap your head into your bag and retain your body heat. Avoid rectangular bags, which are bulkier and harder to pack than mummy bags. Down-filled bags are generally the lightest and most compact bag, but when down gets wet, it will not keep you warm. So, if you select a down bag, pack it in a waterproof, seam-sealed river sack. Synthetic-filled bags are a bit bulkier than down bags, but they usually cost less than down and will still keep you warm after they get wet. Synthetic-filled bags have really improved recently, and now come in a more compact version than their predecessors. When selecting your sleeping bags, avoid the cotton-lined bags. Cotton will not keep you warm when it is wet.

Be aware that, until recently, US sleeping bags were primarily rated using a temperature listing system indicating that you will be comfortable when exposed to the stated temperature rating on the sleeping bag's label. So, if a bag is rated at 20 degrees, you should be comfortable sleeping outdoors if the temperature dips down to 20 degrees. These ratings have been notoriously inconsistent from one brand to another. Several retailers and sleeping bag manufacturers in the United States are adopting a European rating system, known as EN13537, with the goal of improving the consistency in rating sleeping bags. The bottom line: Visit an outfitter and learn all about the sleeping bags you intend to purchase, and be sure they are designed for the environment in which you plan to hike.

Sleeping Pads

Sleeping pads provide an insulation layer between your body and the ground and will help keep you warm as you sleep, not to mention the comfort they provide. For a cozy night's slumber, be sure to bring a sleeping pad for everyone.

Stoves, Cooking Pots, Spoons, and Cups

You will need a backpacking stove to whip up your kid's mac and cheese dinner or to boil water for a cup of hot cocoa. Visit an outfitter to learn about all of the options. If you plan to spend only a few days hiking, a stove with disposable pressurized canisters is compact and easy to use. However, if you plan on backpacking regularly, you may want to consider a refillable liquid-fuel stove. Hang around some serious long-distance thru-hikers and you might be inclined to use one of their homemade stoves using a pop can and denatured alcohol. If you plan on hiking outside the United States, you should acquire a liquid-fuel stove that can burn an assortment of fuels, allowing you flexibility of available resources. There are many stove options to consider. An outfitter that specializes in hiking will help you make the right choice for your hiking needs. You will also need a lightweight cooking pot, plates or bowls, spoons, and cups for hot beverages.

Tent

You will need a lightweight backpacking tent that can accommodate everyone. Get acclimated with your tent before your trip so you're not fumbling with directions while everyone is standing in the rain. Practice setting it up and taking it down in the backyard. Make sure the tent fits into your backpack.

Rope, Bear Bag, or Canister

Chances are you will be hiking in bear country or in an area that will require you to secure your food and all scented items (toothpaste, lotions, and so on) out of the reach of bears and other animals. Many western US parks require the use of a bear canister. Another option in forested areas is to hang your items in a bear bag at least ten feet off the ground between two trees. This will require a fifty-foot length of rope. Research the requirements in the area in which you're hiking and plan accordingly.

EVEN SEASONED HIKERS with all the right gear and experience make mistakes. A few years after walking the Appalachian Trail, prior to having our children, my wife and I hiked the John Muir Trail (JMT), over 218 miles across the Sierra Nevada, in California. We started our journey in Yosemite National Park and walked south through Kings Canyon and Sequoia National Park, ending on the summit of Mount Whitney, the highest mountain in the contiguous United States. On the first day of our expedition, we caught a national park shuttle bus to the trailhead and hiked up from Yosemite Valley to Sunrise camp. We had ascended thousands of feet in elevation that first day. We were about eight miles up the mountain when it began to rain, and we stopped to put on our rain parkas. As I rifled through my pack, I realized our bag of clothes was missing. When we boarded the Yosemite Valley shuttle bus to the trailhead that morning, we carried our clothing bags in one hand and our packs in the other. I knew instantly that I had left one clothing bag on the bus. You need all the right clothing in the High Sierra due to the possibility of quickly changing weather conditions. The mountain range we were hiking in could toss out snow, sleet, hail, and rain unannounced. We pitched camp for the night and studied some maps. The next morning, we hiked on to Tuolumne Meadows—our last opportunity to access civilization—and caught a Yosemite National Park shuttle bus down the mountain to the lost and found. Sure enough, my bag of clothes was waiting for me. After an all-day bus excursion down the mountain and back, we had retrieved the missing clothes and continued our trek of the entire JMT.

A trail as demanding as the JMT is a journey best left for your older teenager. What this story highlights is that even a hiking pro forgets things. When hiking with children, we need to be extra vigilant to make sure we have packed all the necessary gear before hitting the trail.

John Mitchell, photographer

13

Hike with a Team

Utilize the Amazing Services and Resources Offered by
Our Parks and Trail Associations

Planning a hiking adventure with kids can be over-whelming, especially if you are a new parent or a beginning hiker. But with a seasoned outdoor staff and lots of other resources at your fingertips, planning your hike can be as fun as the adventure itself. If you don't know which trail to take, you're unsure if water is available, you're looking for ideas to kick your adventure up a notch to appeal to your older child, or you want to expose your students to an adventure they will never forget, your national park system and trail organizations can help you with all of this and more. Having spent most of my hiking life in the Great Smoky Mountains National Park (GSMNP), the Shenandoah National Park (SNP), and along the Appalachian Trail

(AT), I thought it would be helpful to showcase some of the ways these specific parks and organizations encourage and help with youth and family hiking as of this printing. My experiences with the park trails and staff in the GSMNP, the SNP, and on the AT have reaffirmed the knowledge that our parks and trail associations are chock-full of staff bursting with passion and resources to help you turn a hike into an inspiring grand adventure that your kids will never forget.

Our national parks all have many excellent programs in place for trip planning and engaging our kids in the outdoors. From Acadia National Park in Maine to Yosemite National Park in California and all those in between, you will discover some great resources. Your first stop for information, literally at your fingertips, is the National Park Service website: www.nps.gov. From here you can select the park you plan to visit and pull up detailed information including maps, programs, history, and more. The national parks offer Junior Ranger programs, information for teachers, and plenty of other educational and adventure opportunities specific to each destination. You can participate in the National Park Passport program, which adds excitement to exploring all of our great parks and monuments.

The SNP in Virginia offers lots of hiking adventure opportunities for kids and families, from ranger-led interpretive programs to summer youth programs, ranger-led walks and hikes, and more. You can pick up a copy of Kat and John LaFevre's *Scavenger Hike Adventures: Shenandoah National Park* and explore many of the park's highlights as a family. The park boasts over five hundred miles of hiking trails, including over one hundred miles of the Appalachian Trail. Over the last few years I've worked closely with the SNP ranger staff from the interpretation and education division in a collaborative effort to provide a "Get Your Kids Hiking" program. I've been amazed at the dedication and passion that drives the park staff.

SNP ranger Tim Taglauer had this to say: "Today's youth are tomorrow's caretakers of Shenandoah National Park. So one of our significant goals is to reconnect children and their families with the natural wonders and stories of America's heritage that can be experienced in national parks. We strive to provide a variety of ways to learn about this national treasure through safe, fun-filled adventures that kids of all ages will enjoy. As an example of what can be accomplished, Shenandoah National Park partnered with Northern Virginia Community College to host a summer camp for kids from urban areas in northern Virginia. For many, this was their very first time in a national park. The campers were awed by the mountaintop views, the sunset, the stars, wildlife sightings, and the quiet! One camper summed up her experience: 'This place is special because it shows how beautiful life is, not how ugly it is. It makes you want to make a difference in life and for the greater good.' In the end, we hope that such experiences will lead to a deeper appreciation for national parks and inspire young people to actively care for the parks, their own communities, and the environment."

The GSMNP, one of the most visited of all our nation's parks, kicked off a new "Hike the Smokies for Families" program that rewards families with stickers and pins as they chalk up the miles. Each hiker records his or her hikes in a *Hike the Smokies for Families* booklet and checks in with park rangers to receive stickers. With eight hundred miles of hiking trails, including over seventy miles of the Appalachian Trail, you certainly have lots of trails on which to rack up quality miles with your loved ones. Like many national parks, the GSMNP offers ranger-led interpretive programs, summer youth programs, ranger-led walks and hikes, and more. Pick up a copy of Kat and John LaFevre's *Scavenger Hike Adventures: Great Smoky Mountains National Park* to discover park treasures as you hike along. It was during a family trip to the GSMNP when I was a young teenager that I backpacked for the first time on the Appalachian Trail, planting the seed that inspired me to hike the entire trail later.

I walked the AT and authored a book about my journey, *A Walk for Sunshine*. Through my adventure and book, I've come to know several of the staff at the Appalachian Trail Conservancy (ATC), many of whom have hiked the AT themselves. The AT is the most famous long-distance foot-path in the United States, if not the world. With over a million setting foot on this trail every year, you can bet they have resources in place to engage our kids! In addition to having an easily accessible website (www.appalachiantrail.org), the ATC has several programs in place to inspire future AT hikers and stewards.

In 2006, the ATC and the National Park Service introduced a Trail to Every Classroom (TTEC) to engage youth, promote healthy lifestyles, and preserve our volunteer tradition. This multidisciplinary professional development program for K–12 teachers uses the AT as a valued, local educational resource. Their strategy combines the best practices of place-based education and service learning. This approach builds relevancy and sustainability by focusing on a child's sense of place and civic engagement locally to then build connections to and understanding of national and global issues. Place-based education and service learning is an effective method of teaching that combines academic classroom curriculum with community service. TTEC engages approximately fifty teachers annually, and is offered for five graduate credits. As this program enters its seventh year, they have trained three hundred teachers and community partners, and through the curriculum developed as part of TTEC, they have engaged approximately twenty thousand students.

In 2011, the ATC launched Family Hiking Day. This annual event invites families to take a hike on the AT. ATC invites people of all ages and hiking abilities to get outside and experience the adventure of being active on the trail. Studies show that children are spending less time outside each year, and ATC is working to reverse that trend. Held on National Public Lands Day and coordinating with the Let's Move! initiative, Family Hiking Day is an opportunity to introduce children and families of all ages to America's premier footpath, and all of the benefits that come from being active and spending time outdoors. ATC developed a family program manual and provides resources, including a list of guided hikes led by local volunteers, guidelines for planning a family hike, games and activities for the trail, and a place on their website for the public to submit their Family Hiking Day stories.

In 2012, Girl Scouts USA celebrated their one hundredth anniversary by having Girl Scouts from all over the country hike the AT in sections, starting on March 12, 2012 (the anniversary of the first Girl Scout meeting), and ending on October 31, 2012 (Girl Scout USA founder Juliette Gordon Low's birthday). The goal of the Great Girl Scout Hike was to have every section of the AT, from Maine to Georgia, hiked by Girl Scouts "in bits and pieces." The event's honorary chair, Mary "Mama Boots" Sands, inspired this celebratory hike. Girl Scouts are hoping to get more girls and women out hiking and enjoying the outdoors. ATC was happy to help promote and support their initiative.

The SNP, the GSMNP, and the AT are just a sampling of the twenty-two national parks and thousands of miles of national scenic trails that you can explore with your kids, not to mention the countless state and city parks, forests, and trails. Park officials, park associations, trail clubs, and park concessionaires across the nation have made a point to reach out to families and children. Most parks have helpful websites that serve as great starting points to obtain information about your next hiking adventure.

SHENANDOAH PARK RANGER Georgette Vougias led a group of junior high teenagers from a nearby school on a day hike up to the top of Stony Man, the second-highest peak in the park at 3,765 feet, with a bird's-eye view of the Shenandoah Valley and the Allegheny Mountains. Ranger Vougias's goal for this hike was to help the teens develop a personal connection with the park wilderness. At the onset of their adventure, the students were provided with a worksheet and asked to list any plants and animals they observed. Ranger Vougias took notice of one of the girls in the group, who appeared disengaged based on comments she had been making to her classmates and the things she was writing on her worksheet. The girl's paper was riddled with comments like "gross," "boring," "thing," and "other." Ranger Vougias thought for sure that this girl was not going to make a connection with nature on this outing. Determined to stay focused on the objective, Ranger Vougias continued on, leading the group one and a half miles up the mountain to the summit of Stony Man. With breathtaking views in every direction, Ranger Vougias instructed the students to remain silent for three minutes and take in the experience. She asked the students to write down their thoughts while perched high atop Stony Man. What happened next reaffirmed to Ranger Vougias that her mission to inspire the students to make a connection with the outdoors was not a lost cause. That same girl that led Ranger Vougias to believe that she really could care less about what she was experiencing in the Shenandoah wilderness was transformed. Here are some of the girl's notes written on top of Stony Man that day: "It's like I've entered a fairy tale. . . . There are so many things I haven't seen. . . . Three days isn't enough to take it all in. I've never seen such high mountains. This is the most beautiful national park I have ever been to." The girl's note caught Ranger Vougias by surprise. This young teenager ended up making a powerful connection with the park, which demonstrates how a dedicated park ranger can impact the life of a child by introducing her to our natural world. I'm sure this girl will return again, perhaps with a family of her own one day.

14

Not Me, but Us

Thoughts for Seasoned Hikers and
All Caregivers Hiking with Kids

Hiking with children can turn even the most seasoned hiker and caregiver into a novice, and that's what makes this such a fun adventure! If, prior to children, you've walked long distances, climbed mountains, and gone after your wildest outdoor dreams, you're probably already hooked on the endless possibilities for exploring the great outdoors. Maybe you had no involvement with hiking, but you excelled in golf, ran marathons, achieved your black belt in karate, or you simply excelled in life without children. Hiking aside, many first-time parents experience the anxiety of losing their freedom when children come along.

This anxiety might be downright fear if you are someone who enjoys the freedom of the open trail. Some of this fear may stem from priorities that shift from "me" or "us" to "our children," and, like all endeavors that involve children, your approach to hiking will require a philosophical shift when you hit the trail with your little ones. Don't forget, however, that you also need to find time for yourself, your relationship with your spouse or partner, and your own physical and mental well-being. When you hike a trail for the first time, even as you are enjoying the journey, you are also adapting and overcoming the obstacles along the way. Raising kids, while also maintaining your sense of freedom, is very much like a challenging hike. You want to enjoy the experience while also navigating all the obstacles. Each time you hit the same path, it gets easier and easier.

Some suggested that my days of trekking would end with the birth of my first child. Not so. True, children, especially very young children, require your complete focus. I admit that I had some initial fear that my days of trail freedom were behind me. But after experiencing the triumph of completing the Appalachian Trail solo and the John Muir Trail with my wife, I made a decision not to shelve future adventures for fatherhood. This meant including my child in my adventurous lifestyle. In the summer of 2006, my wife, extended family, and I trekked fifty miles across Ireland. My then twenty-one-month-old daughter and my four-year-old nephew came along. My pace and my trail vocabulary changed from "Do you want to hike another ten miles?" "Where's that mountain ridge with a view?" "Here's the trail to the summit" to "Do you want your sippy cup?" "Where's your pacifier?" "Here, have a Goldfish cracker." Yet, taking my family on a safe outdoor adventure was worth the small sacrifices of adapting to hiking with children. Walking as a family was a priceless bonding experience. The trip included nine other family members as Madison traveled with her aunts, uncles, and grandparents, creating some special memories. We were able to share our hiking passion with our child, and her smile told us that it was worth every step. We all had fun. By the time my son was born in 2007, I was thrilled to add another child to our family hiking adventures. Letting our children experience our outdoor pursuits and dreams will help guide them to their own dreams and passions.

I've come to realize that it's my role as a parent to help my child appreciate the simple things that only nature can provide. On a hike in the Shenandoah National Park with my wife and daughter, we found ourselves splashing in a waterfall instead of following our plan to hike out to a vista. My daughter had a ball, and she couldn't have cared less about the view that we never reached. On my thru-hike, I thought of nothing besides myself and the miles ahead of me, but hiking with children requires an attitude adjustment. Cutting back the distance has actually increased the mileage of happiness. The summit will be there for a future hike. My kids are potential future thru-hikers and stewards of our parks. I want them to have many positive and fun hikes in the woods so that they have a warm foundation to build upon when they think back to their family outdoor adventures.

A good friend I met in my university martial arts club had achieved one of the highest degrees of black belt possible. Then one day he left the martial art in which he had become a master and switched to a completely different martial art, starting over as a white-belted beginner. Other than the white *gi*, his new martial art had major technique and philosophical differences from his previous art. He worked through those differences quickly, and he now holds black-belt status in two different martial arts. After acquiring the basic philosophical differences, my friend was able to apply the same discipline, passion, and even some of the skills from his previous art into his new skill set. The same holds true when you go from hiking without kids to hiking with kids. At first, you may feel like a novice, but after you adjust your hiking philosophy to "them" not "me," all of your previous outdoor experiences will fall into place and become useful skills on your family hikes. All the expertise you acquired and used on your adventures prior to kids, will come to great use as you introduce your child to hiking. You may just need to retool and slow down your approach, and the benefits will be huge.

You can be a great parent and still get your "freedom of the trail" fix. While raising your children, you still need to take care of your own needs. Those first few years of intensive child-rearing chores can sometimes cause us parents to neglect our own well-being. You have to find a balance between your complete focus on caring for your child and taking care of yourself. Without your own health, you will be unable to hit the trail with your kids. Keep in mind, kids grow up fast and will require less time-consuming care as they grow, but if you neglect your own needs, you can fall out of shape and develop health issues that will limit your ability to be a hiking caregiver. Make sure you exercise, eat healthy, and continue to get the necessary sleep your body requires. Gyms offer day care, which could free you up to fit in a hiking-related or cross-training workout. All of us need time to ourselves. When you need a mental escape onto the trail, post a picture from your last adventure as your screen saver. Slip in a nature CD and let your mind drift to that place on the trail.

If taking a solo hike is something you need to do, then do it. Leaving on a six-month adventure along the Appalachian Trail may not be an option during those first few months and years of parenting, but you can still break away for shorter excursions. Even a two-hour hike in a nearby park can provide the hiking fix you need. You and your spouse can take turns taking care of the kids, freeing up each other's time to get your hiking workout in or to simply have some downtime. Perhaps your spouse or partner would like to join you. Our parents have joined us on several vacations, and they did what grandparents love to do—spend time with their grandkids, which allowed Beth and me alone time to slip onto the trail for a more strenuous hike than what we could do with the kids. These little trail escapes help us maintain our relationship. Tap into your parents, extended family, or friends to help with the kids and break away for a mini-vacation. A three-day hike or a weeklong backpacking trip to a national park can soothe those trail-freedom cravings and allow you some healthy downtime from your parenting routine to rekindle your trail romance. If that's not possible, network with other parents in your community with similar hiking interests. Join a local hiking club. Look for family hiking groups in your area on Meetup.com. You will soon discover other families with whom you can plan some joint adventures. While on those adventures you can take turns watching each other's children, allowing each set of parents and caregivers time away to hike or do whatever you like away from kids.

Relish your new role as the parent or caregiver of grand hiking adventures. Dwelling on the end of your pre-kid adventures can bring you down. Focus on the present. Raising kids is a priceless adventure in and of itself. On your pre-kid hiking adventures, you most likely persevered through many unique situations such as preventing hypothermia, fording a river, keeping your water supply topped off, surviving a bear encounter, and more. Raising kids into hikers requires the same problem-solving skills that you used on all your journeys on the trail and in life. Hiking with your kids gives you a natural time to really communicate and build your relationship while removed from the hustle and bustle of everyday life. As soon as your child is able to write, encourage him to journal about your adventures. I keep a journal of all our extended hikes. It's fun to go back and relive the memories. Committing yourself to taking your kids hiking from birth to adulthood requires the same perseverance of a hiker walking from Georgia to Maine. Each day presents a new challenge to adapt and overcome.

Starting your kids out young and hiking together all through their childhood will develop healthy, well-rounded kids. The quality time spent as a family on the trail will be priceless. Teaching your kids to enjoy the simple wonders of the outdoors and building their confidence with each challenging adventure will help them discover their own dreams and passions, whatever they may be. Your time spent hiking with your child will be here and gone with the blink of an eye. Hiking is a holistic athletic endeavor that your kids can use as a tool to navigate through life. If they need time to reflect or a good workout or a fun activity to do with their own kids one day, hiking is a sport that will stand the test of time. Who knows? During these years of hiking with your kids, you might inspire them to become your partner on your next long-distance adventure, or your kids might inspire you to come along on one of their grand adventures in the future. Hiking with your child may be one of the most powerful gifts you can give your kids. Happy trails!

Glossary

The terms defined here may have differing meanings in other contexts. The definitions given here are in direct reference to hiking.

backcountry A term used to describe remote areas of parks that are usually accessible only by foot, horse, or pack animal.

base camp A term used loosely in the hiking community to describe your home away from home where you stage day hikes and other adventures. A base camp provides shelter, food, and amenities and can be a campsite, lodge, cabin, hotel, or wherever you establish temporary residence. Base camps allow you to pack light on your hike but have creature comforts after a day of adventure. Serious mountain climbers, such as those climbing Mount Everest, will use base camps to rest and acclimate to the altitude.

bear canister A bear-resistant container hikers use to keep food and scented items in. Bear canisters are mandatory when backpacking in some parks. These cylinder-shaped containers are made of a hard plastic resin. They offer hikers more camping options without the need of having to secure your food cache by hanging it from trees or bear poles or stowing it inside bear boxes.

bear pole A metal staff placed at some backcountry campsites to secure your food cache high up and out of reach from bears.

carabiner An oblong D-shaped metal clasp with a spring-loaded lever that is often used to quickly attach two items or rope together. Carabiners can be used with rope to hang a bear bag high up between two trees, out of reach from animals, or to secure a climbing harness.

fording a stream To cross a stream at a shallow spot that allows a hiker good footing. Fording a stream requires some skill, especially with fast-moving mountain streams. An Internet search will pull up several video examples.

gaiters An outer layer of waterproof, breathable fabric that wraps around your boot and covers your sock to help keep your feet dry in wet weather. Gaiters also aid in keeping trail debris from getting into your boots.

geocaching A treasure-hunt game that involves the use of a GPS to find and hide containers, known as caches. This game is played by all ages all over the world. The official website: www.geocaching.com.

hiking boots Above-the-ankle footwear with a sturdy sole designed to handle rugged terrain. Hiking boots are available with waterproof, breathable technology and are made from leather or fabric. Hiking boots are made of a lighter material than traditional backpacking and mountaineering boots. Hiking boots are designed for day hikes and short backpacking excursions. The trend toward lightweight products has increased the use of lightweight hiking boots in circumstances where heavy-duty backpacking boots were once used. Hiking boots provide some support from rolling your ankles and minimal break-in time.

hiking shoes Low-cut (below-the-ankle) hiking shoes that are designed with a sturdy sole to protect your foot from impacting injuries from rocks, roots, and uneven trails. Trail shoes have a tread pattern similar to a traditional above-the-ankle hiking boot. They are available with or without the waterproof, breathable material. Trail shoes have become the footwear of choice for long-distance hikers because they are lightweight and durable, though the low cut increases your risk of rolling your ankle.

letterboxing A treasure-hunt game that involves hiking and following clues to locate hidden letterboxes. The Letterboxing North America website: www.letterboxing.org.

metro park A park that is maintained and owned by a city.

national forest A multiuse forest owned by the federal government. National forests serve to preserve the forest while also allowing various activities such as hiking, fishing, hunting, logging, cattle grazing, and more. National forests are managed by forest rangers from the US Forest Service.

national park Maintained by park rangers from the National Park Service, the main purpose of national parks is to preserve and protect natural and historic areas for future generations. National parks limit the use of the area as part of their preservation role. Logging, hunting, and anything other than recreational use is not allowed.

national scenic trail A long-distance trail protected by the federal government for outdoor recreation. National scenic trails often pass through national parks, national forests, state parks, and metro parks.

orienteering A competitive sport that involves the use of a topographical map and compass to navigate in unfamiliar terrain. This is a great way to become efficient with a map and compass for hiking.

shakedown hike A "dry run" training hike using all the equipment you plan to take on your extended adventure. A shakedown hike is meant to make sure everything works and to allow you the opportunity to correct any gear problems and make adjustments *before* you hit the trail. A shakedown hike could be as simple as hiking through the neighborhood and camping in the backyard for the night or hiking overnight to a nearby destination. The idea is to make sure everything fits, the stove works, the water filter pumps, the meals you're planning to cook please everyone's palate, and everyone is comfortably able to carry their gear. This is the best time to discover any gear issues, before you reach your hiking destination.

state park A park that is maintained and owned by the state.

trekking poles Commonly used by seasoned hikers for balance, support, and rhythm while hiking. Trekking poles look like ski poles but have specially designed tips for hiking terrain. Trekking poles can increase a hiker's speed. They provide stabilization when ascending mountainous terrain and aid in controlling your speed when descending. Trekking poles turn hiking into a whole-body workout by distributing the workout to your upper body.

Appendix 1

Day-Hiking Gear Checklist for the Caregiver

Some of the heavy, bulky items can be dispersed among other caregivers and seasoned hiking teenagers. This list should be used in conjunction with the age-appropriate gear lists for children.

DAY-HIKING GEAR LIST

- ☐ Backpack
- ☐ Hydration hose system and/or BPA-free bottles
- ☐ Water filter or treatment system
- ☐ First-aid kit
- ☐ Duct tape (two feet for emergency repairs)
- ☐ Compass
- ☐ Map/topography map
- ☐ Magnifying lens or glasses to read map
- ☐ GPS
- ☐ Whistle
- ☐ Signal mirror

- ☐ Matches and lighter

- ☐ Swiss Army knife or multipurpose knife

- ☐ Survival/locking blade knife

- ☐ Headlamp/flashlight

- ☐ Pedometer

- ☐ Watch

- ☐ Sealable waterproof bags (to keep gear and clothes in)

- ☐ Water

- ☐ Food/snacks (enough for the day plus an extra day of food for emergency use)

- ☐ Personal-hygiene products

- ☐ Hand sanitizer

- ☐ Wet wipes

- ☐ Biodegradable soap

- ☐ Toilet paper

- ☐ Bandanna

- ☐ Sunscreen

- ☐ Sunglasses

- ☐ Bug repellent (DEET or picaridin)

- ☐ Bear spray

- ☐ Plastic spade shovel (for digging your cat hole)

- ☐ Hiking poles

- ☐ Camera

- ☐ Paper and pen

- ☐ Book
- ☐ Repair kits
- ☐ Batteries
- ☐ Cell phone and charger
- ☐ Park emergency phone number

CLOTHING: NON COTTON!

- ☐ Layers of synthetics, wool, and fleece, and waterproof, breathable outer shell
- ☐ Appropriate dress for the weather conditions
- ☐ Extra sets of clothes
- ☐ Base layer
- ☐ Underwear
- ☐ T-shirt
- ☐ Socks
- ☐ Long underwear

INSULATING LAYER

- ☐ Shorts
- ☐ Zip-off long pants/shorts
- ☐ Shirt
- ☐ Fleece jacket or pullover
- ☐ Wool jacket or pullover

OUTER LAYER

- ☐ Rain jacket or parka (waterproof, breathable)
- ☐ Rain pants (waterproof, breathable)
- ☐ Gaiters
- ☐ Hat with brim
- ☐ Hat (fleece or wool)
- ☐ Gloves
- ☐ Boots or trail shoes (make sure they fit)
- ☐ Sandals or Crocs

KEEP IT FUN!

Put your best foot forward to make every hike a safe, fun-filled adventure of a lifetime!

Appendix 2

Backpacking Gear Checklist for the Caregiver

The heavy, bulky items can be dispersed among other care-givers and seasoned hiking teenagers. This list should be used in conjunction with the gear lists for children.

BACKPACKING GEAR LIST

- ☐ Tent
- ☐ Sleeping bag
- ☐ Sleeping pad
- ☐ Backpack
- ☐ Stove (one-burner backpack stove)
- ☐ Cooking pot
- ☐ Spoon
- ☐ Mug for hot beverages
- ☐ Hydration hose system and/or BPA-free bottles
- ☐ Water filter or treatment system

- ☐ Rope, fifty feet (to hang bear bag)
- ☐ First-aid kit
- ☐ Pack cover
- ☐ Duct tape (two feet for emergency repairs)
- ☐ Compass
- ☐ Map/topography map
- ☐ Magnifying lens or glasses to read map
- ☐ GPS
- ☐ Whistle
- ☐ Signal mirror
- ☐ Matches and lighter
- ☐ Swiss Army knife or multipurpose knife
- ☐ Survival/locking-blade knife
- ☐ Water
- ☐ Food (enough for three meals each day plus snacks and an extra day of food for emergency use)
- ☐ Personal-hygiene products
  - ☐ Toothbrush
  - ☐ Toothpaste
  - ☐ Hand sanitizer
  - ☐ Wet wipes
  - ☐ Biodegradable soap
  - ☐ Toilet paper
  - ☐ Bandanna
  - ☐ Vitamins
- ☐ Headlamp/flashlight
- ☐ Pedometer

- ☐ Watch
- ☐ Sealable waterproof bags (to keep gear and clothes in)
- ☐ Sunscreen
- ☐ Sunglasses
- ☐ Bug repellent (DEET or picaridin)
- ☐ Bear spray
- ☐ Plastic spade shovel (for digging your cat hole)
- ☐ Hiking poles
- ☐ Camera
- ☐ Paper and pen
- ☐ Book
- ☐ Repair kits
- ☐ Batteries
- ☐ Cell phone and charger
- ☐ Park emergency phone number

CLOTHING: NON COTTON!

- ☐ Layers of synthetics, wool, and fleece, and waterproof, breathable outer shell
- ☐ Appropriate dress for the weather conditions
- ☐ Extra sets of clothes

Base Layer

- ☐ Underwear
- ☐ T-shirt

- ☐ Socks (2–3 pairs)
- ☐ Long underwear

Insulating Layer

- ☐ Shorts
- ☐ Zip-off long pants/shorts
- ☐ Shirt (1 for day; 1 for night)
- ☐ Fleece jacket or pullover
- ☐ Wool jacket or pullover

Outer Layer

- ☐ Rain jacket or parka (waterproof, breathable)
- ☐ Rain pants (waterproof, breathable)
- ☐ Gaiters
- ☐ Hat with brim
- ☐ Hat (fleece or wool)
- ☐ Gloves
- ☐ Boots or trail shoes (make sure they fit)
- ☐ Sandals or Crocs

KEEP IT FUN!

Put your best foot forward to make every hike a safe, fun-filled adventure of a lifetime!

Appendix 3

Gear Checklist for the Birth to Six-Month-Old Hiker

This list should be used in conjunction with the caregiver gear checklist. The items listed are suggested items to pack along for your infant.

GEAR

- ☐ Infant carrier
- ☐ Stroller (for extended trips)
- ☐ Insect repellent (DEET or picaridin—2 months and older)
- ☐ Sunglasses
    - ☐ Bug net for infants under 2 months
- ☐ Travel wipes and case
- ☐ Milk bottles
- ☐ Formula
- ☐ Pacifiers
- ☐ First-aid kit

- ☐ Hand warmers
- ☐ Baby medicine (baby pain reliever)
- ☐ Medicine for allergic reactions (Benadryl)
- ☐ Thermometer
- ☐ Trail toys
  - ☐ Rattle
  - ☐ Bells
  - ☐ Stuffed animal
  - ☐ Small mirror

DIAPER-CHANGING KIT

- ☐ Diapers—pack enough for each day of your trip.
  - ☐ Pack extra
- ☐ Diaper-rash cream
- ☐ Changing pad
- ☐ Wet towelettes
- ☐ Tissues
- ☐ Hand sanitizer
- ☐ Trash bags for dirty diapers

CLOTHING: NON COTTON!

- ☐ Layers of synthetics, fleece, and wool, and waterproof, breathable clothing
- ☐ Appropriate dress for the weather conditions
- ☐ Extra sets of clothes

BASE LAYER

- ☐ Synthetic one-piece with feet
- ☐ Synthetic or wool socks

INSULATING LAYER

- ☐ Fleece one-piece with feet and a hood
- ☐ Shirt
- ☐ Pants
- ☐ Shorts

OUTER LAYER

- ☐ Waterproof, breathable rain parka
- ☐ Fleece mittens or synthetic socks for hands
- ☐ Fleece hat
- ☐ Brimmed sun hat

Appendix 4

Gear Checklist for the
Six- to Thirty-Six-Month-Old Hiker

This list should be used in conjunction with the caregiver gear checklist.

GEAR

- ☐ Child carrier
- ☐ Stroller (for extended trips)
- ☐ Insect repellent (DEET or picaridin)
- ☐ Sunscreen
- ☐ Lip balm
- ☐ Sunglasses
- ☐ Travel wipes and case
- ☐ Sippy cup
- ☐ Water
- ☐ Snacks
- ☐ Lunch food

- ☐ Pacifiers

- ☐ First-aid kit

- ☐ Hand warmers

- ☐ Baby medicine (baby pain reliever)

- ☐ Medicine for allergic reactions (Benadryl)

- ☐ Thermometer

- ☐ Playful items to tie from a shoestring onto the child carrier
  - ☐ Pacifier
  - ☐ Play binoculars
  - ☐ Play compass
  - ☐ Favorite small toy
  - ☐ Books related to the outdoors
  - ☐ Toy or play camera

DIAPER-CHANGING KIT

- ☐ Diapers—pack enough for each day of your trip
  - ☐ Pack extra

- ☐ Diaper-rash cream

- ☐ Changing pad

- ☐ Wet towelettes

- ☐ Tissue

- ☐ Hand sanitizer

- ☐ Trash bags for dirty diapers

• • •

CLOTHING: NON-COTTON!

- ☐ Layers of synthetics, fleece, and wool, and a waterproof, breathable outer shell
- ☐ Appropriate dress for the weather conditions
- ☐ Extra sets of clothes

BASE LAYER

- ☐ Synthetic top and bottom
- ☐ Synthetic or wool socks
- ☐ Synthetic long underwear

INSULATING LAYER

- ☐ Fleece or wool jacket (midweight or expedition weight, depending on weather)
- ☐ Shirt
- ☐ Pants
- ☐ Fleece pants
- ☐ Shorts
- ☐ Water-resistant trail shoes or tennis shoes

OUTER LAYER

- ☐ Waterproof, breathable rain parka or jacket
- ☐ Waterproof, breathable rain pants
- ☐ Fleece mittens or gloves
- ☐ Waterproof gloves or mittens

- ☐ Fleece hat
- ☐ Brimmed sun hat
- ☐ Rain boots

Appendix 5

Gear Checklist for the Three- to Four-Year-Old Hiker

This list should be used in conjunction with the caregiver gear checklist.

GEAR

- ☐ Adventure pack
- ☐ Folding umbrella stroller (for extended trips)
- ☐ Child carrier—if size and weight still appropriate
- ☐ Insect repellent (DEET or picaridin)
- ☐ Sunscreen
- ☐ Lip balm
- ☐ Sunglasses
- ☐ Travel wipes and case
- ☐ Disposable training pants
- ☐ Hand sanitizer

- ☐ Tissues
- ☐ Trash bag for dirty disposable training pants
- ☐ BPA-free water bottle
- ☐ Water
- ☐ Snacks
- ☐ Lunch food
- ☐ First-aid kit
- ☐ Hand warmers
- ☐ Child medicine (baby pain reliever)
- ☐ Medicine for allergic reactions (Benadryl)
- ☐ Thermometer
- ☐ Adventure pack items
  - ☐ Play binoculars
  - ☐ Play compass
  - ☐ Favorite small toy
  - ☐ Books related to the outdoors
  - ☐ Kids' camera
  - ☐ Bug catcher
  - ☐ Magnifying glass
  - ☐ Water bottle

CLOTHING: NON COTTON!

- ☐ Layers of synthetics, fleece, and wool, and a waterproof, breathable outer shell
- ☐ Appropriate dress for the weather conditions
- ☐ Extra sets of clothes

Base Layer

- ☐ Synthetic top and bottom
- ☐ Synthetic or wool socks
- ☐ Synthetic long underwear

Insulating Layer

- ☐ Fleece or wool jacket (midweight or expedition weight, depending on weather)
- ☐ Shirt
- ☐ Pants
- ☐ Fleece pants
- ☐ Shorts
- ☐ Water-resistant trail boots, shoes, or tennis shoes

Outer Layer

- ☐ Waterproof, breathable rain parka or jacket
- ☐ Waterproof, breathable rain pants
- ☐ Fleece mittens or gloves
- ☐ Waterproof gloves or mittens
- ☐ Fleece hat
- ☐ Brimmed sun hat
- ☐ Rain boots

Appendix 6

Day-Hiking Gear Checklist for the Five- to Twelve-Year-Old

This list should be used in conjunction with the adult caregiver day-hiking gear list (appendix 1). Your child may not be able to carry all of the items. Some of the items listed are also on the caregiver gear list. You can eliminate duplicate items to downsize your child's pack weight.

DAY-HIKING GEAR LIST

- ☐ Backpack
- ☐ Hydration hose system and/or BPA-free bottles
- ☐ Water
- ☐ Food/snacks (enough for the day plus an extra day of food for emergency use)
- ☐ First-aid kit
- ☐ Child medicine (pain reliever)
- ☐ Medicine for allergic reactions (Benadryl)
- ☐ Prescription medicine

- ☐ Personal-hygiene products
  - ☐ Hand sanitizer
  - ☐ Toilet paper
  - ☐ Tissues
  - ☐ Travel wipes and case
- ☐ Insect repellent (DEET or picaridin)
- ☐ Sunscreen
- ☐ Lip balm
- ☐ Sunglasses

CLOTHING: NON COTTON!

- ☐ Layers of synthetics, wool, and fleece, and a waterproof, breathable outer shell
- ☐ Appropriate dress for the weather conditions
- ☐ Extra sets of clothes

BASE LAYER

- ☐ Underwear
- ☐ T-shirt
- ☐ Socks
- ☐ Long underwear

INSULATING LAYER

- ☐ Shorts
- ☐ Zip-off long pants/shorts
- ☐ Shirt
- ☐ Fleece jacket or pullover

☐ Wool jacket or pullover

OUTER LAYER

☐ Rain jacket or parka (waterproof, breathable)

☐ Rain pants (waterproof, breathable)

☐ Gaiters

☐ Hat with brim

☐ Hat (fleece or wool)

☐ Gloves

☐ Boots or trail shoes

ADVENTURE/SURVIVAL ITEMS

These will vary based on age and interest. The following is a list of suggested items.

☐ Compass

☐ Map

☐ GPS

☐ Pedometer

☐ Whistle

☐ Signal mirror

☐ Headlamp/flashlight

☐ Binoculars

☐ Small toy

☐ Books related to the outdoors

☐ Camera

- ☐ Bug catcher
- ☐ Magnifying glass
- ☐ Plastic spade shovel (for digging your cat hole)
- ☐ Hiking poles
- ☐ Paper and pen

Appendix 7

Backpacking Gear Checklist for the Five- to Twelve-Year-Old

This list should be used in conjunction with the adult caregiver backpacking gear list (appendix 1). Your child may not be able to carry all of the items. Remember, a child should carry no more than 20 percent of his or her body weight. Some of the items listed are also on the caregiver gear list. You can eliminate duplicate items to downsize your child's pack weight.

BACKPACKING GEAR LIST

- ☐ Backpack
- ☐ Pack cover
- ☐ Sleeping bag
- ☐ Sleeping pad
- ☐ Hydration hose system and/or BPA-free bottles
- ☐ Sealable waterproof bags (to keep gear and clothes in)
- ☐ Water

- ☐ Food/snacks (enough food for three meals a day plus snacks and an extra day of food for emergency use)

- ☐ First-aid kit

- ☐ Spoon

- ☐ Bowl

- ☐ Mug for hot beverages

- ☐ Child medicine (pain reliever/prescriptions)

- ☐ Medicine for allergic reactions (Benadryl)

- ☐ Personal hygiene products
  - ☐ Hand sanitizer
  - ☐ Toilet paper
  - ☐ Tissues
  - ☐ Travel wipes and case
  - ☐ Biodegradable soap
  - ☐ Vitamins

- ☐ Insect repellent (DEET or picaridin)

- ☐ Sunscreen

- ☐ Lip balm

- ☐ Sunglasses

CLOTHING: NON COTTON!

- ☐ Layers of synthetics, wool, and fleece, and a waterproof, breathable outer shell

- ☐ Appropriate dress for the weather conditions

- ☐ Extra sets of clothes

Base Layer

- ☐ Underwear (2–3 pairs)

- ☐ T-shirt (2–3 pairs)

- ☐ Socks (2–3 pairs)

- ☐ Long underwear top and bottom (2 pairs)

Insulating Layer

- ☐ Shorts

- ☐ Zip-off long pants/shorts

- ☐ Shirt

- ☐ Fleece or wool jacket or pullover (midweight or expedition weight, depending on weather)

Outer Layer

- ☐ Rain jacket or parka (waterproof, breathable)

- ☐ Rain pants (waterproof, breathable)

- ☐ Gaiters

- ☐ Hat with brim

- ☐ Hat (fleece or wool)

- ☐ Gloves

- ☐ Boots or trail shoes

- ☐ Sandals or Crocs

Adventure/Survival Items

These will vary based on age and interest. The following is a list of suggested items.

- ☐ Compass

- ☐ Map/topography map

- ☐ GPS
- ☐ Whistle
- ☐ Signal mirror
- ☐ Headlamp/flashlight
- ☐ Plastic spade shovel (for digging your cat hole)
- ☐ Binoculars
- ☐ Small toy
- ☐ Books related to the outdoors
- ☐ Camera
- ☐ Bug catcher
- ☐ Magnifying glass
- ☐ Pedometer
- ☐ Watch
- ☐ Hiking poles
- ☐ Paper and pen

Appendix 8

Day-Hiking Gear Checklist for the Thirteen- to Eighteen-Year-Old

This list is very similar to the adult caregiver list except that some of the essential and recommended items may not be appropriate for minors and should be in the possession or supervision of the adult caregiver.

DAY-HIKING GEAR LIST

- ☐ Backpack
- ☐ Hydration hose system and/or BPA-free bottles
- ☐ Water filter or treatment system
- ☐ First-aid kit
- ☐ Hand warmers
- ☐ Duct tape (two feet for emergency repairs)
- ☐ Compass
- ☐ Map/topography map
- ☐ Magnifying lens or glasses to read map

- ☐ GPS
- ☐ Whistle
- ☐ Signal mirror
- ☐ Headlamp/flashlight
- ☐ Pedometer
- ☐ Watch
- ☐ Sealable waterproof bags (to keep gear and clothes in)
- ☐ Water
- ☐ Food/snacks (enough for the day plus an extra day of food for emergency use)
- ☐ Personal-hygiene products
  - ☐ Hand sanitizer
  - ☐ Wet wipes
  - ☐ Biodegradable soap
  - ☐ Toilet paper
  - ☐ Bandanna
  - ☐ Vitamins
- ☐ Sunscreen
- ☐ Sunglasses
- ☐ Bug repellent (DEET or picaridin)
- ☐ Plastic spade shovel (for digging your cat hole)
- ☐ Hiking poles
- ☐ Camera
- ☐ Paper and pen
- ☐ Book
- ☐ Repair kits

- ☐ Batteries
- ☐ Cell phone and charger
- ☐ Park emergency phone number

CLOTHING: NON-COTTON!

- ☐ Layers of synthetics, wool, and fleece, and a waterproof, breathable outer shell
- ☐ Appropriate dress for the weather conditions
- ☐ Extra sets of clothes

Base Layer

- ☐ Underwear
- ☐ T-shirt
- ☐ Socks
- ☐ Long underwear

Insulating Layer

- ☐ Shorts
- ☐ Zip-off long pants/shorts
- ☐ Shirt
- ☐ Fleece jacket or pullover
- ☐ Wool jacket or pullover

Outer Layer

- ☐ Rain jacket or parka (waterproof, breathable)
- ☐ Rain pants (waterproof, breathable)
- ☐ Gaiters

- ☐ Hat with brim

- ☐ Hat (fleece or wool)

- ☐ Gloves

- ☐ Boots or trail shoes (make sure they fit)

- ☐ Sandals or Crocs

Items That Should Be in Possession or Supervision of an Adult Caregiver

- ☐ Bear spray (keep out of reach of children)

- ☐ Matches and lighter

- ☐ Swiss Army knife or multipurpose knife

- ☐ Survival/locking-blade knife

- ☐ First-aid medicine

Appendix 9

Backpacking Gear Checklist for the Thirteen- to Eighteen-Year-Old

This list is very similar to the adult caregiver list except that some of the essential and recommended items may not be appropriate for minors and should be in the possession or supervision of the adult caregiver.

BACKPACKING GEAR LIST

- ☐ Tent
- ☐ Sleeping bag
- ☐ Sleeping pad
- ☐ Backpack
- ☐ Cooking pot
- ☐ Spoon
- ☐ Mug for hot beverages
- ☐ Hydration hose system and/or BPA-free bottles
- ☐ Water filter or treatment system

- ☐ Rope, fifty feet (to hang bear bag)
- ☐ First-aid kit
- ☐ Hand warmers
- ☐ Pack cover
- ☐ Duct tape (two feet for emergency repairs)
- ☐ Compass
- ☐ Map/topography map
- ☐ Magnifying lens or glasses to read map
- ☐ GPS
- ☐ Whistle
- ☐ Signal mirror
- ☐ Water
- ☐ Food (enough for three meals each day plus snacks and an extra day of food for emergency use)
- ☐ Personal-hygiene products
  - ☐ Toothbrush
  - ☐ Toothpaste
  - ☐ Hand sanitizer
  - ☐ Wet wipes
  - ☐ Biodegradable soap
  - ☐ Toilet paper
  - ☐ Bandanna
  - ☐ Vitamins
- ☐ Headlamp/flashlight
- ☐ Pedometer
- ☐ Watch
- ☐ Sealable waterproof bags (to keep gear and clothes in)

- ☐ Sunscreen

- ☐ Sunglasses

- ☐ Bug repellent (DEET or picaridin)

- ☐ Plastic spade shovel (for digging your cat hole)

- ☐ Hiking poles

- ☐ Camera

- ☐ Paper and pen

- ☐ Book

- ☐ Repair kits

- ☐ Batteries

- ☐ Cell phone and charger

- ☐ Park emergency phone number

CLOTHING: NON-COTTON!

- ☐ Layers of synthetics, wool, and fleece, and a waterproof, breathable outer shell

- ☐ Appropriate dress for the weather conditions

- ☐ Extra sets of clothes

Base Layer

- ☐ Underwear (2–3 pairs)

- ☐ T-shirt (2–3 pairs)

- ☐ Socks (2–3 pairs)

- ☐ Long underwear top and bottom (2 pairs)

• • •

Insulating Layer

- ☐ Shorts
- ☐ Zip-off long pants/shorts
- ☐ Shirt (2–3 shirts)
- ☐ Fleece jacket or pullover
- ☐ Wool jacket or pullover

Outer Layer

- ☐ Rain jacket or parka (waterproof, breathable)
- ☐ Rain pants (waterproof, breathable)
- ☐ Gaiters
- ☐ Hat with brim
- ☐ Hat (fleece or wool)
- ☐ Gloves
- ☐ Boots or trail shoes (make sure they fit)
- ☐ Sandals or Crocs

Items That Should Be in Possession or Supervision of an Adult Caregiver

- ☐ Bear spray (keep out of reach of children)
- ☐ Matches and lighter
- ☐ Swiss Army knife or multipurpose knife
- ☐ Survival/locking-blade knife
- ☐ Stove (one-burner backpack stove)
- ☐ First-aid medicine

Appendix 10

First-Aid Kit

This is a suggested list to consider as you prepare your first-aid kit. You may add items to accommodate everyone in your hiking party.

FIRST-AID KIT

You can purchase a first-aid kit to accommodate the number of hikers in your group and then add items specific to your group (for example, prescriptions and allergy medications).

- ☐ Antibiotic ointment
- ☐ Antiseptic wipes
- ☐ Sterile gloves
- ☐ Bandage assortment
    - ☐ Large quantity of standard size for all the kids' cuts and scrapes
    - ☐ Butterfly
    - ☐ Large bandages
    - ☐ Little bandages
    - ☐ Gauze dressing roll

- ☐ Gauze pads
- ☐ Safety pin
- ☐ Medical tape
- ☐ Moleskin for blisters
- ☐ Scissors to cut moleskin and gauze
- ☐ Tweezers for splinters
- ☐ Tick remover
- ☐ Hand warmers
- ☐ Foot warmers
- ☐ Emergency foil blanket
- ☐ Cold pack
- ☐ Thermometer
- ☐ After Bite
- ☐ Anti-itch cream (hydrocortisone)
- ☐ Anti-fungal cream
- ☐ Burn cream
- ☐ Ibuprofen (Advil)
- ☐ Naproxen sodium (Aleve)
- ☐ Children's pain medicine
    - ☐ Acetaminophen
    - ☐ Ibuprofen
- ☐ Antihistamine (diphenhydramine, e.g., Benadryl)
- ☐ Rehydration salts for dehydration
- ☐ Prescriptions

- [ ] Allergy medicine
  - [ ] EpiPen
- [ ] First-aid guide/manual
- [ ] Park emergency phone number
- [ ] Paper and pen

Appendix 11

"Take a Hike" Song Lyrics

This song was written by Jeff Alt as a fun way to encourage kids and the whole family to hit the trail. Alt, his wife, two children, and his father, dressed as a bear, have performed a family "Take a Hike" dance with slides. Music is a great way to share hiking tips.

TAKE A HIKE

© 2010 Composed and recorded by Todd Alt
Vocals and Instrumentals by Todd Alt
Lyrics Written by Jeff Alt

—LYRICS—

Sitting on the couch and your belly is growing a pouch, take a hike.
Take a hike.
Kids are out of school and you don't know what to do, take a hike.
Take a hike.
Feeling kind of stressed and your life is a mess, take hike.
Take a hike.

Want to think outside the box, can't think outside your
socks, take a hike. Take a hike.

Let's all go and take a hike.
Come on, let's take a hike.

Going to hit the trail and you don't know what to do, seek advice.
Let's take a hike

The children take the lead and the parents take the tail, on the trail.
Take a hike.
You're dressed in non cotton layers, plenty of food and water,
on the trail. Take a hike.
Be sure to wear the right shoes or your feet will be singing the blues
on the trail. Take a hike. To protect the plants and animals and
prevent from getting lost, stay on the trail, on the trail.
Leaves of three, let them be, on the trail. Take a hike.
Sometimes it rains and pours but there's always campfires and
s'mores, on the trail.

Let's take a hike.
Let's all go and take a hike.
Grab your boots and take a hike.

Mother Nature has a way of taking your breath away, in the woods.
Let's take a hike.
You start to look around, it's all so simple yet profound,
in the woods. Take a hike.
The smell of earth and plants, natural sights at every glance,
in the woods. Take a hike.
You're away from all distractions, you begin to find
satisfaction, in the woods. Take a hike.
You start to focus on each other, it's nice to have everyone together.
Let's take a hike.

Let's all go and take a hike!
Come on let's take a hike.
Grab your boots and take a hike.
Come on let's take a hike!

Suggested Reading

Alt, Jeff. *A Walk for Sunshine: A 2,160-Mile Expedition for Charity on the Appalachian Trail.* 3rd ed. Cincinnati: Dreams Shared, 2009.

Apel, Kenn, and Julie Masterson. *Beyond Baby Talk: From Sounds to Sentences; A Parent's Complete Guide to Language Development.* Roseville, CA: Prima Publishing, 2001.

Biddulph, Steve. *Raising Boys: Why Boys are Different—and How to Help Them Become Happy and Well-Balanced Men.* Berkeley, CA: Celestial Arts, 1998.

Brunelle, Lynn. *Camp Out! The Ultimate Kids' Guide.* New York: Workman, 2007.

Carline, Jan D., Martha J. Lentz, and Steven C. Macdonald. *Mountaineering First Aid: A Guide to Accident Response and First Aid Care.* 5th ed. Seattle: Mountaineers Books, 2004.

Elium, Don, and Jeanne Elium. *Raising a Son: Parents and the Making of a Healthy Man.* 3rd ed. Berkeley, CA: Celestial Arts, 2004.

Kjellström, Björn, and Carina Kjellström Elgin. *Be Expert with Map and Compass: The Complete Orienteering Handbook.* 3rd ed. Hoboken, NJ: Wiley, 2009.

Kuffner, Trish. *The Preschooler's Busy Book: 365 Creative Games and Activities to Keep Your 3- to 6-Year-Old Busy.* Minnetonka, MN: Meadowbrook, 1998.

———. *The Toddler's Busy Book: 365 Creative Games and Activities to Keep Your 1 1/2- to 3-Year-Old Busy*. Minnetonka, MN: Meadowbrook, 1999.

LaFevre, Kat, and John LaFevre. *Scavenger Hike Adventures: Great Smoky Mountains National Park*. Guilford, CT: Globe Pequot, 2007.

———. *Scavenger Hike Adventures: Shenandoah National Park*. Luray, VA: The Shenandoah National Park Association, 2009.

Louv, Richard. *Last Child in the Woods: Saving Our Children from Nature-Deficit Disorder*. Chapel Hill, NC: Algonquin, 2005.

Masarie, Kathy, Jody Bellant Scheer, and Kathy Keller Jones. *Raising Our Daughters: The Ultimate Parenting Guide for Healthy Girls and Thriving Families*. Portland, OR: Family Empowerment Network, 2009.

Meeker, Meg. *Strong Fathers, Strong Daughters: 10 Secrets Every Father Should Know*. New York: Ballantine, 2007.

Mountaineers, The. *Mountaineering: The Freedom of the Hills*. 8th ed. Seattle: Mountaineers Books, 2010.

Murkoff, Heidi, Arlene Eisenberg, and Sandee Hathaway. *What to Expect the First Year*. New York: Workman, 2003.

———. *What to Expect the Toddler Years*. New York: Workman, 1996.

Savedge, Jenn. *The Green Parent: A Kid-Friendly Guide to Earth-Friendly Living*. Seattle: Kedzie, 2008.

Resource List

The companies, retailers, and organizations listed here may help as you acquire all the gear and knowledge to get your kids hiking.

BACKPACK AND DAY PACK BRANDS WITH KID SIZES

Deuter: www.deuter.com
Eastern Mountain Sports: www.ems.com
Kelty: www.kelty.com
Mountain Smith: www.mountainsmith.com
Osprey: www.ospreypacks.com
REI: www.rei.com

BEAR SAFETY PRODUCTS

Bear Keg—Bear-Resistant Food Container:
    http://counterassault.com
Counter Assault Bear Deterrent—Bear Pepper Spray:
    http://counterassault.com

BUG REPELLENTS AND RELATED ACCESSORIES

AfterBite, to soothe a bug bite: www.tendercorp.com
Ben's DEET insect repellents: www.tendercorp.com

Coghlan's infant mosquito net: www.coghlans.com
Natrapel picaridin insect repellents: www.tendercorp.com
Sawyer brand permethrin insect repellent for clothing: www.
sawyer.com

CHILD CARRIERS

BabyBjörn: One of the most widely used infant carrier
brands, available in a moisture-wicking fabric:
www.babybjorn.com/us
Ergobaby infant carriers: http://store.ergobaby.com
Kelty Kids: A popular brand of child carriers, day packs,
and backpacks. Kelty brand is widely available at hiking
equipment retailers. www.kelty.com
Deuter: A respected brand of kid carriers and kid packs,
carried by many retailers. www.deuter.com
Osprey child carriers: www.ospreypacks.com

COMPASS

Suunto: www.suunto.com

DRY SACKS (FOR STORING CLOTHING)

Outdoor Research ditty bags and dry sacks:
www.outdoorresearch.com

FIRST AID

Adventure Medical Kits' Family First Aid:
www.adventuremedicalkits.com

Wilderness first aid, administering first aid when help is delayed, wilderness first responder, and CPR training are all excellent skills to have. The following are a few agencies that offer
wilderness first-aid training:

- National Outdoor Leadership School (NOLS):
  www.nols.edu/wmi/courses/wildfirstaid.shtml
- Red Cross: www.redcross.org
- Wilderness First Aid: http://wfa.net

FOOD FOR HIKING AND BACKPACKING THAT YOUR KIDS MAY ENJOY

Clif Bar: http://clifbar.com
Backpacker's Pantry—freeze-dried food:
    www.backpackerspantry.com
Enertia Trail Foods: http://trailfoods.com
Mountain House—freeze-dried meals:
    www.mountainhouse.com
Natural High—freeze-dried food: www.richmoor.com

FOOTWEAR FOR KIDS

Hi-Tec: www.hi-tec.com/us
Keen: www.keenfootwear.com/us/en
Lowa: www.lowaboots.com
Merrell: www.merrell.com
New Balance: www.newbalance.com
Teva: www.teva.com

GLOBAL POSITIONING SYSTEMS (GPS) AND RELATED PRODUCTS

Amber Alert GPS—a tracking system if you are concerned
    your child might get lost: www.amberalertgps.com
Garmin—GPS: www.garmin.com/us
Optimal Tracking—GPS system if you are concerned your child
    might get lost: www.optimaltracking.com/en
SPOT Satellite GPS Messenger—this device uses satellite

communication to initiate a rescue with a push of a button: www.findmespot.com

HEADLAMPS

Petzel headlamps: www.petzl.com/us
Princeton Tec headlamp: www.princetontec.com

KITCHEN SUPPLIES FOR THE BACKCOUNTRY

MSR Whisperlite International—lightweight backpacking stove: http://cascadedesigns.com
MSR PocketRocket—ultralight compact backpacking stove: http://cascadedesigns.com
MSR MugMate coffee/tea filter: http://cascadedesigns.com
MSR Titan titanium cup: http://cascadedesigns.com
MSR Titan two-pot set—lightweight titanium cook set: http://cascadedesigns.com
GSI Outdoors utensils: www.gsioutdoors.com

KNIVES FOR HIKERS

Swiss Army knife: www.swissarmy.com/us
Gerber folding, locking-blade survival knife: www.gerber-tools.com

LEAVE NO TRACE SEVEN PRINCIPLES .

The Leave No Trace seven principles—Leave No Trace Center for Outdoor Ethics: P.O. Box 997 Boulder, CO 80306, (800) 332-4100 www.lnt.org

OUTDOOR CLOTHING FOR KIDS

Bridgedale socks: www.bridgedale.com
Columbia—all clothing layers: www.columbia.com
Helly Hansen—outer layers: www.hellyhansen.com

Marmot: http://marmot.com

Outdoor Research—gaiters and hats:
www.outdoorresearch.com

Patagonia: www.patagonia.com/us

REI: www.rei.com

The North Face: www.thenorthface.com

SmartWool socks: www.smartwool.com

OUTDOOR RETAILERS

There are many local and regional outfitters that specialize in hiking equipment—far more than I could even begin to list. Here are a few national outdoor retailers that carry hiking clothing and gear for kids.

- Campmor: www.campmor.com
- Eastern Mountain Sports: www.ems.com
- REI: www.rei.com

REGULATORY AND HEALTH ORGANIZATIONS
THAT PROVIDE CHILDREN'S HEALTH AND SAFETY ADVICE

American Academy of Pediatrics (AAP)—"Dedicated to the Health of Children": www.aap.org

Centers for Disease Control and Prevention (CDC):
www.cdc.gov

Environmental Protection Agency (EPA): http://epa.gov

Skin Cancer Foundation—sun protection: www.skincancer.org

SLEEPING BAGS IN KID SIZES

Kelty: www.kelty.com Mountain Hardware: www.
mountainhardwear.com

The North Face: www.thenorthface.com

Sierra Designs: www.sierradesigns.com

Slumberjack: http://slumberjack.com

Marmot: http://marmot.com

SLEEPING PADS

Kelty: www.kelty.com
Therm-a-Rest: http://cascadedesigns.com/therm-a-rest

STROLLERS

Babies"R"Us umbrella strollers—durable and compact, a useful item when trekking with an infant from town to town: www.toysrus.com
BOB—multiuse and jogging strollers:
   www.bobgear.com/revolutionse
Kelty—jogging strollers: www.kelty.com

SUNSCREEN PRODUCTS FOR KIDS

Coppertone Water Babies—broad-spectrum, water-resistant,
   SPF 50: www.coppertone.com
Coppertone Kids—broad-spectrum, water-resistant, SPF 50:
   www.coppertone.com
Neutrogena Pure and Free Baby Sunblock Stick—for facial
   areas: www.neutrogena.com

TENTS FOR FAMILY BACKPACKING

Big Agnes: www.bigagnes.com
Kelty: www.kelty.com
Marmot: http://marmot.com
Mountain Hardware: www.mountainhardwear.com
Sierra Designs: www.sierradesigns.com

TREKKING POLE BRANDS WITH KID SIZES

Black Diamond: www.blackdiamondequipment.com LEKI:

www.leki.com

WATER

CamelBak hydration systems: www.camelbak.com
Coghlan's iodine water treatment tablets: www.coghlans.com
Katadyn water filters: www.katadyn.com
Nalgene water bottles: http://nalgene.com
Platypus hydration systems: http://cascadedesigns.com
SteriPEN—ultraviolet-light water treatment:
    www.steripen.com

WEIGH YOUR GEAR

An online site that allows you to weigh your gear:
    www.weighmygear.com

Acknowledgments

I would like to thank my publisher, Beaufort Books, and especially Eric Kampmann, Margot Atwell, Megan Trank, and Cindy Peng for assembling *Get Your Kids Hiking* into this book and getting it into the hands of families and caregivers.

Get Your Kids Hiking was years in the making, and it would not have been possible without the help, support, and talent of countless family, friends, outdoor professionals, book publicists, and more.

What began as a personal quest to get my own kids hiking at a very young age ended up bringing my family and friends together in a fun, outdoorsy way. So many family and friends have joined us on our kid hikes in the Great Smoky Mountains National Park, the Shenandoah National Park (SNP), and even Ireland. These hikes not only built great memories and instilled the outdoor spirit in our children but also allowed me to field-test many of the hiking-with-kids techniques in this book. All this wouldn't have been possible without my wife, Beth, and children, Madison and William, for literally putting their best steps forward and going along with my adventure plans. I would like to thank several of our family members and friends who have joined us on family hikes over the years: Mike and Sue Alt; Ron and Rose Almendinger; Laur and Kathy Richards; Larry, Greta, Alec, and Elena Kuykendall; Todd and Stefanie Alt; Dan, Stephanie, Dylan, and Drew Pitts; Steve, Kiara, and Chris Almendinger; Mark, Dawn, Alyssa, and Kaitlyn Shoviak; Brian, Liz, Sean, and Cade Osborn; Tom, Tommy, Corey, Conner, and Chase Parris; Jason, Julie, Mike, Molly, and Erin Szucs; Ed, Brenda, and Alexander Foos; and Brycen, Lisa, Alexa John, and Anya Hudock.

I soon realized that other families could benefit from my tips for hiking with kids, which evolved into the implementation of a Get Your Kids Hiking program for SNP visitors. Since I already had an established program in the SNP about my *Walk for Sunshine* Appalachian Trail journey, I presented my hiking-with-kids idea, and it quickly became a program in the SNP. I would like to thank Helen Morton and Nick Smith of Aramark for making it possible for me to collaborate with the SNP ranger staff in the creation of a hiking-with-kids program. I would like to thank the SNP ranger staff specifically—Tim Taglauer, Regina Cardwell, Georgette Vougias, and several more park rangers—for committing time and resources to offer a collaborative Get Your Kids Hiking program, making this event a successful park venue.

For several years and with the help of family and friends, I've presented various hiking-with-kids programs as part of the award-winning annual Wilderness Wildlife Week (WWW) Convention in Pigeon Forge, Tennessee. Our presentations have included a song produced by my brother, and I've even gotten my dad to dress up as a black bear onstage. This venue has allowed me to practice articulating my *Get Your Kids Hiking* tips before a fun and interactive audience. I would like to thank Butch Helton and Brandon Barnes of the Pigeon Forge office of special events for allowing us to share these hiking tips with other families at WWW. I would like to thank the following family and friends, who have served as cast and crew during these events: Mike and Sue Alt; Kathy and Laur Richards; Todd Alt; Dan, Stephanie, Dylan, and Drew Pitts; Jason, Julie, Mike, Molly, and Erin Szucs; and, of course, my own wife and kids, Beth, Madison, and William Alt.

I would like to thank one of my book publicists, Paul Krupin, for encouraging me to write an article jam-packed with all my fun tips to get children hiking. This article generated significant interest and was published in magazines, newspapers, blogs, and on several prominent websites across the United States and in Canada and Sweden. The article even led to several radio and TV bookings. This astounding response is what motivated me to expand my tips into this book. I would like to thank my friend and colleague, Kay Pfeifer, a pediatric and school based occupational therapist and mother of two, for contributing her expertise on facilitating the outdoor sensory experience in the my chapter, Everyone has a place on the trail. I would like to thank my friend Julie Szucs, an instructor at Miami University and also a mother of three active, outdoor children, for her willingness to read through my first manuscript draft and provide her editing advice. When you're close to a project, you can sometimes miss some technical details. I would like to thank my friend Bill Dietzer, a hiking instructor, presenter, and trail guide, for catching some of those minor details and for providing his technical advice as I assembled my manuscript. I would like to thank Greta Miller, from the Shenandoah National Park Association, and Steve Kemp, from the Great

Smoky Mountains Association, for reviewing portions of my manuscript for accuracy.

I'm especially grateful for all of the great outdoor opportunities that exist through our national, state, and local park and trail organizations, including similar outdoor venues across the globe. What I've found is that many of the parks and trails that I've visited wouldn't be what they are without the countless volunteers who exert a deep passion in the preservation of the great outdoors. Thank you!

Index